THE
QUARTERLY

EDITED BY

GORDON LISH

HOB BROUN, WHOSE FICTIONS "ROSELLA, IN STAGES" AND "THE BLOOD ASPENS" APPEARED IN Q2 AND Q3, RESPECTIVELY, DIED 15 DECEMBER 1987, OF HEART FAILURE. MR. BROUN WAS THIRTY-SEVEN YEARS OLD, AND HAD BEEN PARALYZED AS A RESULT OF LIFE-SAVING SPINAL SURGERY UNDERTAKEN WHEN HE WAS THIRTY. HE BREATHED WITH THE ASSISTANCE OF A RESPIRATOR, AND PRODUCED WRITING BY OPERATING A SIP-AND-PUFF DEVICE THAT ACTIVATED A FRANKLIN ACE 2000 COMPUTER. IT WAS BY THESE MEANS THAT MR. BROUN COMPOSED HIS NOVEL *Inner Tube*—AND HIS FORTHCOMING COLLECTION OF STORIES *Cardinal Numbers*. THERE WAS A LONG WORK OF PROSE—*Wild Coast*—IN PROGRESS WHEN MR. BROUN SUCCUMBED. PRIOR TO HIS PARALYSIS, HOB BROUN HAD BROUGHT OUT THE NOVEL *Odditorium*. THE EDITOR OF THIS MAGAZINE KEPT UP A SOMETIME CORRESPONDENCE WITH HOB BROUN AND WITH HIS MOTHER AND FATHER, JANE AND HEYWOOD HALE BROUN, AND CAN POINT TO NO BRAVER PEOPLE. THIS EDITION OF *The Quarterly* IS DEDICATED TO THE BROUN FAMILY—ONE WANTS TO SAY THE BROUN FAMILY—WHOSE EXAMPLE SHALL NOT PERISH.

THE
QUARTERLY

5 / SPRING 1988

VINTAGE BOOKS

A DIVISION OF RANDOM HOUSE

NEW YORK

ALL RIGHTS RESERVED UNDER INTERNATIONAL AND PAN-AMERICAN
COPYRIGHT CONVENTIONS. PUBLISHED IN THE UNITED STATES
BY RANDOM HOUSE, NEW YORK, AND SIMULTANEOUSLY
IN CANADA BY RANDOM HOUSE OF CANADA LIMITED, TORONTO.

THE QUARTERLY (ISSN 0893-3103) IS EDITED BY GORDON LISH
AND IS PUBLISHED IN MARCH, JUNE, SEPTEMBER, AND DECEMBER
FOR $28 THE YEAR ($42 IN CANADA) BY VINTAGE BOOKS,
A DIVISION OF RANDOM HOUSE, INC., 201 EAST 50TH STREET,
NEW YORK, NY 10022. APPLICATION TO MAIL AT SECOND-CLASS
POSTAGE RATES IS PENDING AT NEW YORK, NY, AND AT ADDITIONAL
MAILING OFFICES. SEND ORDERS AND ADDRESS CHANGES TO
THE QUARTERLY, VINTAGE BOOKS, SUBSCRIPTION DEPARTMENT,
ELEVENTH FLOOR, 201 EAST 50TH STREET, NEW YORK, NY 10022.
THE QUARTERLY WELCOMES THE OPPORTUNITY TO READ WORK
OF EVERY CHARACTER, AND IS ESPECIALLY CONCERNED TO KEEP
ITSELF AN OPEN FORUM. MANUSCRIPTS MUST BE
ACCOMPANIED BY THE CUSTOMARY RETURN MATERIALS,
AND SHOULD BE ADDRESSED TO THE EDITOR, THE QUARTERLY,
201 EAST 50TH STREET, NEW YORK, NY 10022. THE QUARTERLY
MAKES THE UTMOST EFFORT TO OFFER ITS RESPONSE TO
MANUSCRIPTS NO LATER THAN ONE WEEK SUBSEQUENT
TO RECEIPT. OPINIONS EXPRESSED HEREIN ARE NOT NECESSARILY
THOSE OF THE EDITOR OR OF THE PUBLISHER.

ISBN: 0-394-75718-1

DESIGN BY ANDREW ROBERTS
MANAGEMENT BY DENISE STEWART AND ELLEN F. TORRON

MANUFACTURED IN THE UNITED STATES OF AMERICA

PAULETTE JILES, TED PEJOVICH, YANNICK MURPHY, MARK RICHARD,
JENNIFER ALLEN, PETER CHRISTOPHER, SHARON DUPREE, AND
WILLIAM TESTER WILL READ FROM THEIR WORK THE EVENING OF
22 APRIL, BEGINNING AT 8 P.M., THIS UNDER THE AUSPICES OF
THE WRITER'S VOICE, IN THE AUDITORIUM OF THE WESTSIDE Y,
AT 2 WEST 64, NYC, WITH GORDON LISH INTRODUCING.
FOR TICKET INFORMATION, TELEPHONE 212-787-6557.

THE QUARTERLY

5 / SPRING 1988

THE QUARTERLY

THE

QUARTERLY

Part of the crowd

Sea Girls and Men with Hands

Winter Sundays at Boneyard Cove you can come see the fishermen's women, how these women sit with blanketed shoulders on fold-up wooden chairs set along the rocks at low tide where the white salt waters hit the barnacled hull of the fishermen's boat, the *Sea Girl*. These two women, the two of what six winter storms back was three women who came here, I saw the day after the fishermen's boat ran the jut of rocks, how these three women all swam out into the turning waters as the Coast Guard air-horned of riptide undertows, how these women kept on until one and then another came treading in a crawl back onto the rocky shore, the first carrying the torn flag of the *Sea Girl,* the second a knotted fishnet, and the third, this woman, she was lifted by rope out of the waters onto the Coast Guard boat's wide deck as it motored tall waves away out of Boneyard Cove.

This Sunday, today, after an all-night foghorn/foglight every hour on the half-hour watch, I walk the dirt path down the cliff to Boneyard Cove, sit myself down behind the fisher-men's women's chairs, close enough so the offshore mist moves the flowery taste of perfume my way, close enough so as to hear the woman who has the *Sea Girl* flag scarved over her hair say, "Sure as this is Pacific, my Bill, he is still out there, I am sure of it. Bill is out there on that island, being fed homemade mayonnaise to by a native beauty with hair all the way down to her heels, under the shade of a coconut palm."

"Island, what island?" the other woman says, unknotting the fishnet that covers her legs. "There hasn't been an island out there for years."

"Oh, it's out there," the scarved woman says, the woman who now stands as the blanket drops off her shoulders onto the chair. "It's about right over there." She points. "You just can't make it out so well through all this haze."

"You're the haze," the other woman says, unknotting the fishnet with her teeth. "Walk around with that flag on your head, do you know that is authentic hand-painted silk imported back from Fiji by Jim himself? You could make a good dollar or two selling it at the pier bazaar instead of waiting around the dock mailbox how you do all the time waiting for your once-a-month check."

Today the fog banks low into the wishbone curve of Boneyard Cove. A daytime white fog with the sun somewhere above the thick of it all, barely burning through, making your eyes weak to the just-woke-up morning glare. You cannot see beyond the end of the rocks where the swelled waves come in, where the waves rise to hit against the *Sea Girl*'s red-painted hull, salt-worn to a red sort of brown, the brown of the kelp beds that float with the weight of a gull that has just landed there, chewing on a piece of what looks like plastic bag.

"Maybe you're right," the scarved woman says, pushing her sunglasses off onto her head. "Maybe Bill is out in Fiji now, speaking Fijian with the native women dancing around his dick, Bill eating roasted pig from an open fire. It must be night in Fiji. Don't you think it's probably nighttime there now in Fiji? And Bill, I can see him laying his big dick down to rest on a bed of palm leaves."

"Did I tell you, last week's bazaar I got twenty plus off all of those broken brass barometers Jim had hanging out on the porch?" the other woman says, pulling the chopstick out of her tied hair. The woman's hair falls a sun-bleached grayish blond over her blanketed shoulders as she goes at the knots with the chopstick, saying, "When this is done, it will make a hammock for seven or eight easy."

Eight dollars per half-hour watch is what I get for staying awake while standing up, for not falling over and waking with my face pressed against the handled controls, the foghorn/foglight both turned to a flashing red OFF in the where-am-I middle of a night when a winter storm throws water down from the sky and up from the ocean in waves tall enough to clear a bait shack off the end of a pier, tall enough to knock away more than sixty years of standing wood-pier pilings out over the beach sand and through the beachfront glass-window homes.

The scarved woman takes off her sunglasses, rubs the lenses with a ragged end of the *Sea Girl* flag, and, sliding the sunglasses back onto her head, says, "Bill, that tropical sun must be murder on his eyes, a whole day out on the boat and Bill's eyes get so bloodshot red that they actually look greener, like green as, even like, well, those fish—you know all those fish we got the extra freezer for? Like green as those fish bellies are, if you can believe it, Bill's eyes, I've seen them look just so green as that."

"You think if I got this wet, any of this mess would come out any easier?" the other woman says, slipping the chopstick behind her ear. "Jim used to say, what did he say, something about how water makes the hardest work easy—something like that. I can't remember it now, can you?"

I can.

I can remember how these three fishermen I saw from my tower window came walking up the stone steps on a day when there was sun so wide and far for miles that you could see all the way out to where the ocean ended in a mountain of island, how these three men walked side-to-side in a heavy wet-boot way up the stone steps to the door down below, calling out, "Knock, knock, anybody home?" I went running down the spiral stairs, lost a beach sandal along the way, to unbolt the double-iron triple-bolt doors, and opening up, "Christ," said the one with sunglasses on, "got enough locks to hold out a whole drunk ship of Navy," and "Can we come in?" said the other, wearing a *Sea Girl* windbreaker, as the third one walked in, stepping wet on my bare foot, and this third one ran the spiral stairs, soon out of sight, as the one with sunglasses followed after, shouting, "Hot on your wake! Hot on your wake!" and "Jim," said the one with the *Sea Girl* windbreaker, putting out his hand that went what felt like two hands around mine, "the boys here, as you can see, are a bit excited. None of us before has ever gone in a real-life lighthouse. Mind showing us how you work the ropes here?"

So what ropes are there to show of the two-handled controls, what is there really to show to these fishermen, to these men with hands, as I watched one by one each take a pull at the foglight handle, hands built bone-strong to net, reel, lift a deckload of still-flapping fish, hook-cut hands through storms of winter, lightning nights of spring, red-tide dead-fish waters of summer and through the fall, when the winds turn the current oceanward; hands that have worked these men a way to feed a beach town for more years than I have been alive. And what do you say when the one with the sunglasses throws an arm around your neck, pulls you close to his fresh-bait smell, and says, "So you're the mighty lighthouse king," while the third one, with his head out the tower window, says, "Ever think of jumping?"

As I followed the fisherman called Jim, last behind, back down the spiral stairs, he said to me, "If you ever want to come out on the boat sometime, do," and then at the iron door, while the other two men ran on ahead, this man, Jim, he said, "You know, son, it's good to see someone as clean-cut, all-American as yourself—though you're missing a shoe, you know—is up here watching over all us boys down there in the water. You keep up the good work, now," and then Jim gave me a big-handed slap to my shoulder and made his side-to-side way slow down the stone steps.

Fogged days such as this, you can tell time by how high the waters come up over the black rocks, how far the waters now cover the slanted deck, burying the *Sea Girl* name on the bow, making the time somewhere between an hour or less left of day, making also less of a walk from the women's chairs to the water's edge, where the other woman goes dragging the fishnet behind, the fishnet that catches on rocks here and there as the woman keeps on walking, giving a tug here and there until she reaches the tide-pool waters, where she bends, her hair falling over her face as she dips, draws the fishnet in, out of the water, while the scarved woman, she moves back to her wooden chair, pulls the blanket over her shoulders, sits.

"Look here!" shouts the other woman, carrying the fishnet dripping over the stomach of her dress as she lets the fishnet unwind onto the rocks where, caught in between, are needled sea urchins.

The scarved woman takes a sea urchin by one of its needles, drops the urchin onto the rocks, where the needled shell breaks, and, leaning over out of her chair, says, "Bill loves these. You get the egg here, scoop it out like this, and taste," and "No, thanks," says the other woman, "I'm saving mine. I can get five flat a pound off these at the fish market," and "Maybe you're right," says the scarved woman, wiping the egg into the shell, "maybe I should save mine for Bill."

As for me, the mighty lighthouse king, I saved no one in my standing sleep on that winter-storm night when not even the Coast Guard boated out, a night the Navy halted all shell practice at the island for what six years of calm winter has left a strip of sand that disappears down under at high tide, a night the soundless thick of fog comes in around you in your towered soloness, waiting for your half-hour duty call to no one out there anyhow, you think, until the afterstorm of the next day, when you, or I should say I, when I saw the one boat of the only fishermen I ever barely knew in this entire beach town I grew up in is rock-wedged in the point of the cove below, and maybe, I thought, maybe they're not on it, maybe those three fishermen just did not tie the boat up tight to the docks, maybe the boat got shoved loose by the storm and just drifted out on its own into the night, but I knew there was no possible way those fishermen's hands would mis-dock the boat that gave them their ocean living they worked for to have to their very own deaths.

"It's about that time," the other woman says, gathering

the sea urchins into the knotted fishnet, and "Yes," the scarved woman says, "I've got to get this in the freezer," and these women, they take hold of their blankets with both hands, press their chins to the middle of the blankets to fold once, drop twice over their legs, and then place the blankets in the seats of the wooden chairs they close, and I follow.

I follow this one with her chair under her arm, the fishnet slung over her shoulder on her back, and this one, this one with the chair held on her scarved head, up the dirt cliff path of Boneyard Cove to the grassy mound of uppermost land, where I stop.

I stop and watch these two women throw their chairs, and then this one her fishnet, into the flatbed of a truck, where two men sit in the front cab, harpoons hung in the rack behind their black-capped heads, as the women climb in through the opened cab doors, over the men's laps, to a shoulder-to-shoulder seat between the two men, who shut the cab doors, and when the engine starts up, the scarved woman slips the *Sea Girl* flag down off her red-gold hair, and SKINDIVERS DO IT DEEPER on the bumper as the truck drives in a dirt cloud away.

Here is the *Sea Girl*'s rusted anchor sunken in the grass where I saw, six years back, these same two women throw dust over their shoulders off the cliff to the waters of Boneyard Cove, dust that could have been dust of anything but of the fishermen who to this day are somewhere still unfound, out there under the waters that cover the hull of the *Sea Girl*, where gulls waver above, and where now, as on all winter Sundays at this hour at Boneyard Cove, you can see the sun coming through in a fog bow of light—me standing, looking out to the who-knows-how-deep of the ocean's waters to where there are those who are lost at sea, from this point here where there are the those of us who are lost on land. **Q**

Darling

See my brother and my mother and me in the light in our back yard, by the barn and the silver silo rocketed up above the barn, on the farm of what is all there is in the world in my mind? All there is is towered archward of our barn, it seems to me, on the grass, beside the boards, of the fence in our back yard. "See the cowy-cow?" my mother says to me. "See the pretty cow?" Darling looms like something giant in a scary tale; she rubs her butt against the waxy stick of a chinaberry tree beside the barn, making the batch of the leaves on the tree to shake, and some of the leaves to drop and fall like feathers down all around her, and banty hen and chicks at Darling's hooves. Darling is liable to fall on me and crush me on the grass, I think. I look up at her—and all there is—as if from in a pit, the white boards of our fence chalked on the sky, and on the barn the window square and blackly yawing, tugs of straw pinched out between the splitted boards and corners of the barn. My mother lifts me up off of the grass. She crooks my head up and lowers my butt, so I can see what all there is behind our house: our cow, the barns, and, farther out, our clodded, fallow field, brokenly and barren, the tractor in it swollen and coupling something backwards, buggish, rusted-toothed, and over all of this, the leaning, siloed, hard, and cloudless hood of unimportant blue.

Darling lumbers close to us, big-eyed and alive and like a giant toy to me, all whorled and piebald-blotched in black and white. She gives my little arm a sniff; she rubber-noses it, and I feel the warm in Darling's sniff surround my arm and on my chest.

My brother has a pointy limb, and scratches it on Darling. "Cowy-cow," my brother says, and jabs her in her eye with it.

And see how Darling stands as still as a picture of a cow caught in the light in our back yard?

A cow, or horse, or bigger something, shovels with its hooves out in the ground around our house, or in the field— their hulking forms—beside our night yard in the dark. I wake to dark and see my hand there on my pillow like an egg, and think that cows are in our yard again; I imagine fence board cast, or stoven in, the cows upbloated, munching on our lawn.

And dull into a pinchful sleep, terrible with school.

And Daddy's morning voice is out our door, sketching sounds: "You all," and then, "Get up." His voice becomes a dark-armed, overcasting thing in my dream, in the world of how it is when I am almost all awake—when I can't move. When I am scrunching small up in my bed. My brother, Jeab, above me in his bunk, his mattress hump pressed down at me, Jeab awake up in his bed; I know he is; we pretend to be asleep. Cows, or something bigger, hoove the ground, pick at it, shovel up the dirt around my foot.

And Daddy knocks outside our room.

"Boys . . ." he says.

Jeab pushes at the air, and hits the floor, bumping looser laid-out odds and ends, and on our desk, coins, pens, nails shelved in the wall—tremble of the moment, ring. Jeab, his butt before me in the strip of door-crack light in our dark room. "Get up," says Jeab. "Get up," Jeab says. Here, the blackly marble of Jeab's butt lobes in the dark. Jeab is pulling up his pants. Jeab trunks up his cock above his underwear elastic. I close my eyes. Make as if to clear my throat, and cough. I'm half asleep; I have to make a fuss with me to get myself to school.

Momma has her grits and biscuit done, her smoking menthols in our kitchen, and her waitress apron on. Have my place beside her at the table with my eggs, and the eggs have too much grease for me. Everything is grabby-like and pinchy at my eyes. Everything's too big and glared to see. Put a blistered bacon in my mouth, the taste of salt.

Daddy comes into the kitchen with his Stetson in his hand. And the sleep lines scrim my daddy's face. Daddy sees it's me. He hangs his Stetson on his chair. We are all a sleepy fog, save for my brother with his math. My head is of a weakly spring. Daddy asks if I am feeling poorly much this morning. He says, "You boys aren't pulling taters now, when you all got your school, are you?" Momma clicks her cheek at him; she covers her mouth with her cigarette hand and grins. I fork my eggs. Daddy looks up to the table end to nothing in the chair. He says if I am feeling puny, he thinks I should stay in bed. I nod yes to him, and Daddy, he tells Jeab to finish seeding up the scrub and not be bothering me today.

"What?" is what Jeab says to him.

Jeab says what did he do, anyhow, and biscuits at his eggs. Momma combs her hand back of my neck, then takes her hand back to her coffee cup. "Shush," my momma says to my brother, Jeab.

Nothing of this morning seems to fit is what it is. I drink some milk, and go and get back in my bed.

The yellow bus pulls in out front. Talk is outerdoored and in our yard, then our truck, then there is nothing but a rooster and some cows up near our house, and me alone, kneeing curled and in the warm of in my bed, in the dark, and the monsters arming back, and the house is full of haunts that come when we go off to school. I am here with God alone and all there is. Me in small up in my bed. Me and God on our farm of the whole, wide world.

Outside, we have a white gate with a trellis over it knitted through with frozen rose limbs by the fence, between the barn and the scraped landscape of our brown yard; I can see out from my bed onto the windowed afternoon. My bed, of the lower of the bunkbeds, here, in covers. My breath mists on the window in a smudge, then clears into a watered lens, around the day. See our gate out in the day inside the lens.

Something in our living room ticks, like wood, or a foot on wood, or a ghost, which bumps the air down the shadow of our hall walls into my room. Then I hear the tick again as a memory in my head, as of ghosts, or as the devil having conjured in our house, in the almost soundless roaring of the quiet in the air. Our house is holding its breath in here, swollen to the walls. Outside is littered ice and foams of snow still on the ground. Tin lifts in the wind, out on the roof of our gray barn, settles slow. Whistles coil around our house.

I get up to go outside, and stand in the hallway by their door. Momma and Daddy's room is curtain-blue in the window light. Even all their furniture looks blue. And the smell of Momma and Daddy is like the smell of hangered clothes, and of collars, and of closet-darkened smells, and a spongy, spray-can smell of something powdery and lead. A wall of Momma's smell wells up, above my momma and daddy's bed, of her hair, or of a towel that has been used, of talc, and then my daddy's thinner smell in under hers. Daddy's smell is bitterer, and lingers, edged and orange-peelish, from their bed.

Here is Daddy's hard desk chair, and him, or my sense of him, haunting in the chair, in this dimness. See how broad my daddy's rear has worn against the chair—the size of Daddy on the seat!

I ease back the drawer of Momma's perfume-cluttered bureau, a paper box, a lotion tube, this lip-print tissue ball; there are things that they have hidden here, in a spot that moves around, from the closet to the bureau, to the closet, back again. Here, a band with snaps in black elastic, here a wrap of cellophane from something. Momma's drawer has a sort of shoe-store smell of wads and knots of slickened cloth. Dim and tangled cocoa hose; clouded silks and nylons stretch, grit against themselves, catch the cedar board inside the drawer. Here, a fog of nylon stocking, toeing brown around my arm. I move some silk on silk of something between my finger and my thumb. Hold it wadded to my face and smell the wash. My heart throngs like a fever in the blue done in the dark. Hot is mostly up my arms and on my shoulders and my neck. I hear a car go by our house, outside, that isn't ours. I know God or God and something else, is watching in the dark. I sit down across their bed.

Lay on back.

And then I hear the tick again—of wood, or like the sound of something settling in the air about our house. I wrap a baby Coke along with biscuit in my cover, shinny up the cold antenna pole outside our house. I start where the pole is smoothed, and grip where hands have turned the pole to get the television right—I could fall and smash my arm down on the windowsill, I think. A robin darts off from the tiles as I chin up. I'm larger now. I have the feeling I could leap across our yard, and the barns, and if I could just let go enough—all of what there is around our farm—I'm not so small up on the roof; I am out in the airy world again. I have my baby Coke and biscuit breakfast in the sun.

And see how God is sickened in the sun?

This is how it is in our back yard. An almost-path in the icy yard grass where we walk out to the gate. Our red-washed tool-and-feed shed like a playhouse in the yard, last year's Christmas lights still hung on it. The poles of Momma's clothesline leant askew; the bugs of clothespins twitching wire, then the stark white-boarded fence in our back yard. And me and God. And I am like a doll tossed on our roof, and there are ghosts loose in our house and at my back inside our attic. Ghosts are in the ground—ghosts in our barn.

There are cows out anting distant in the field about our farm, black and brown. I watch, and drink my baby Coke, and burp the flavor of a biscuit.

The yellow bus junks up and yaws across our county road;

I can see the heads of school kids in the row of window squares. I fly the distance to our school, past all the houses and the farms, into town, but it's not really there; school appears like in a dream, disappears when I'm not in it in the flesh. Nothing is really *real* but what I see. What is here around our farm.

I see glimpses of the Stoke girl's brassing hair, bunched guitar strings on the window of the bus, the oval red of sweater, shouldered there against the glass. Little children's heads, hands.

And here, my brother, Jeab, again. Not a jacket and nary a sweater on his arms out in the sun. Jeab is upright, down diagonal from me up on the eave. I watch him stalk across the county road, a hero from a Bible tale, his hard jawbone in the out-of-doors, spit there, glistening on the grin on his lips. He stalks past something animal the dogs dragged to our yard, a rag, a shoe, a disk of something flattened tin. Jeab is prince of all of this, he knows he is. He says that this will all be his someday. He takes all of what there is of this as his, by being him, by being bigger and the older one.

The yellow bus junks on to miniature on down our county road.

Our front door bangs shut. Ghosts hie into the closets and the walls inside our house.

—And God remains outside.

I look down around our farm and close my eyes. See the chicken shed done darkly on the inside of my eyes, in the murky-colored space just past my eyelids in the dark. See the things I saw in lighter gone to dark, and the darker things I saw now done in light. I open my eyes and it all goes.

Everything is the same.

In our house some voices clatter like our TV set is on. I hear my brother shout out, "Bub! Hey, Bub!"

But I'm not home. I am flying over all the world I have up in the clouds. Me and God up in the sun.

My brother, Jeab, stalks from our house holding bread. "Yo, Bub," Jeab says. He turns and bites a hunk of half his bread. "Hey, fuck," my brother, Jeab, says to nothing. "Let's get to work."

I watch the top of what is my brother's head. "I am sick," I say to him. Jeab, he turns and looks to where I'm at, up in the sun.

Jeab says, "Do you need anything, Bub?"

"Yeah," I tell him.

"You okay enough to do the cows?" he says.

Jeab puts the rest of his bread into his mouth and goes inside, munches on some sounds which hold his mouth up in his head.

And I am gone in clouds again.

My brother drops his one-nine-ohs.

I can feel it shake the blocks beneath our house, shudder up our slatted walls and through the gable of our kitchen, where a shingle grits my head. Have to turn and watch. Come down on-off our house before our house is shook apart and we are crushed. And I will have to stay here in the wreckage as a ghost, with all the other ghosts inside our house, when I'm alone.

And I will be the ghost that has to make the ticking sounds.

I lay my empty bottle and my blanket on our porch, come around and watch my brother shove his weights into the air, inhale, and blow out spirit from the blowhole of his mouth, and shake the ground. Forty times, or more, out in our yard, out in the sickened, clouded paint washed in the air, no shirt on over my brother's chest, upwedged, and bellowed like a swollen heart, to me, my hands hung in my pockets on the porch. Smell the sweated male of him. Watch. Jeab has a chest on him you want to lick. I can see the Stoke girl licking it, naked on the grass, their lower, adult hair shown in the sun. I should be pushed around by him, or mounted like a dog, have dirt or

cow manure kicked on me—how dogs or bulls will ~~do a smaller~~
dog or a smaller bull.

"Done . . ." says Jeab, his mouth lolling open in a hole, and
Jeab agog around like he was meeting his comers-on.

"Shit," Jeab says. "You coming, Bub?"

"Better not," I say to him. "I have some stuff to do, milk."

"Well, you figure it," says Jeab. "Daddy anywhere?"

"No."

"Well," says Jeab. He pulls his short-sleeved shirt back on.
Foots his weights back in the dirt below our house, says, "No,
don't get up, Bub."

My brother goes.

"No, I won't," I say, and I go inside our house and get my
bucket and a towel. Our tractor winds to start, and spats a
rattling to the walls, and a sound of gears at grinding in the
ground below our house; then our tractor sound is softer, then
is almost all but gone. And the hush of devil sounds are in our
house. I take my blanket to my bed.

In Momma and Daddy's room I check the look of all their
things. Momma's bureau dresser looks the same. The things
on it in coma. I push Daddy's chair into his desk, then pull it
back. I tug at the bedspread on their bed. The devil at their
bedside tugging, too. His breath there on my neck, below my
ear. His smell, the smell of him of sweat and shirt and wash,
as I walk out.

I run water in my bucket and go outside. See the snow in
tatters foaming junk across our yard, the rusted plow round-
edging ice. I unlatch our gate and feel some water pat my hair.
My head wetting slow, in spots of cold, the way that warm
would move around my butt when I would wet my bed. I see
trellis ice and paint shavings wet against the sky; the sun is low,
and water runs the limbs of Momma's roses, either side of our
white gate. If I ease open the gate, I know, the trellis will get
me soaked, so I don't. I bolt. Water falls all over me like rain.

I chain back the gate shut on our yard. Daddy's truck

drives up and throats its gearing down. I am out here in the nick of time. Daddy will see me with my bucket, then he will leave to go help Jeab. And all of what there is that is our farm will just be mine. I will lay down in the light and be with God and fly around. And like a ghost, or like a cow, I will never leave our farm. I will go out where the cows are lying down and be a cow. I will eat our frozen grass just like a cow beside the cows. And I will sleep beside the cows, and never ride our bus to school.

My boots crunch on the glass stems of the frozen grass and weeds. There are black trees on the wire fence, far across our land.

Darling there looms solid-large, waiting in the dark for me.

She moos.

Now my brother, Jeab, and me, in tube light from my kitchen sink. Jeab swings his Navy coat off and shoulders it on his chair back. His clothes are mostly corners, black or white, particolored markings on the front part of his coat. All his gold looks polished. Jeab unsnaps his clip-on tie and rolls it balled into his shirt pocket. He is taller than our daddy is—Jeab looks like Daddy, has our daddy's Irish head. "Good God," Jeab says, "what a wreck." Jeab turns his beer can up and takes the suds; beer drops falling measured in my kitchen's jittering light, drops of beer in foam strobes, sluicing onto my brother's tongue. Jeab presses an hourglass figure in his can, sets it rocking on the tabletop, says, "God, son, what a flophouse."

My brother has his broad white hat up on his lap, across his Navy pants, says, "Gee-ma-fucking-netty, Bub." He grunts. I can taste the way his breath smells in our air.

I ask does he want another cold one.

"Go ahead," says Jeab.

My brother, Jeab, is watching me; he shakes his head. "So you don't give your big brother a hug," he says. "Shit, son."

. . .

My brother, Jeab, is talking about our farm while taking off his uniform, which he folds in creases blockingly, and flat, and puts into his duffel bag next to his chair. Now Jeab is down to undershorts. His legs are tan, hairless as an Amazon's but bigger. Ham slick. Here is the butcher's chart, in cuts of steak above his shins: giblets in his guts and in the sausage of his groin, twirling fur above his groin runs to his heart. Then Jeab is a swimmer in my kitchen in his shorts. He puts on his jeans, and then his T-shirt—*Death from Above,* with its winged skull—his arms above his head, like in a dive. Jeab puts his NAV-TAC baseball cap on his head, thumb-tip bills it level-squared. "Used to ride you on my bike," he says. "You wasn't but this big . . ."

I tell Jeab we worked too much.

Jeab says he doesn't really remember when. "Can you not tell if I'm civilian?" says Jeab to me, billing at his cap.

Here are steaks, and chops, and fat cuttings parceled. Jeab has the Adam's apple of some unlikely lizard in his throat; the freckles on his neck there, mottled as the dots on an apple where the apple stem goes in. Jeab says, "They don't let you fly your sidearm, P.R.P. . . . What kind of guns you got around?"

I tell him I did my part when we were kids.

"Son, get real," says Jeab.

Jeab opens my refrigerator door, and I can hear the motor miss, trundle a moment, stop running. Jeab looks in the refrigerator, then at me.

"It's nothing but some beer in here," says Jeab, "and a egg."

Jeab says, "Now, how are we going to put some pudding on the runt? Huh, son?"

Outside my kitchen window, it starts to rain. A dark spot on the glass, and then another dark spot, and then some smaller dark spots mar the glass, and the water runs outside of my apartment—you can hear it then, rain pouring onto things in tip-tap sounds out in the city's rainy night. I tell my brother we can still go out. Jeab says he doesn't really feel like dressing for a restaurant.

"We can order in," I say.

"Daddy beat hell out of me," says Jeab.

I disagree.

Here is Daddy kissing Jeab, and then my daddy kissing me; Daddy crushing me in his hairing arms and lifting me by my waist like I am just a sack of feed across his back. Knuckled bones pop in my back in Daddy's arms; he jams me stiffly to the ground. My brother, Jeab, has watered, ink-run marks gleamed awash his cheeks. He is crying, and the light shines from the fire on his face. Momma hugs him; then, like she is pouting, smacks his charcoal-sooted arm.

And my daddy kisses Jeab, and me as well, out in the throwdown from the fire on the night.

Jeab has burned our barn down.

"I only have this one, me alone," I say to Jeab.

And I get cauled up in the blankets and the boxes in my closet, tottering my jacket and the hook head of a shroud, of my buttoned-open shirt on a hanger on the pole. The closet door shuts at my heels, and on my clothes.

And I reach for the shoebox with the blue-velvet sack, the kind of sack that once someone had liquor in and drawstrung at the top. And my hand reaches in under the shoebox lid, like your hand in a hole for an egg, or a cat, or a lobster in a hole, or your hand in a closet in the dark. I heft out the sack and feel the lead, and the heavy in my hand is the center of the closet from the lead, as if the lead had done some science to the air, in this dark.

And it is like the gun in my hand by our barn, and the heavy of lead in my hand is the heavy of something alive. My brother, Jeab, walks beside me with his gun, his mackinaw

jacket, and his deer-hunting cap on his head. Jeab draws back
the white door of our barn, and the light is of a party on inside.
Or an ark, and the smell of some cows and some pigs and some
horses and some mules and some chickens and some guineas
and some peahens and some sheep having a party in the ark,
but inside, it is a jumping-bed of hay, and the light of a house,
or a party going on. A yellowy light full of dust on the hay in
the barn, and no animals inside but the three mange dogs
wired tight to the beam at the center of the barn Jeab would
burn.

And its back is a brush on the black standing dog, like it
is braced for a push from a truck, or to water in a tub, and the
hair from the back of the gray-spotted dog is a mouse of some
hair in a clump, on the beam, where the gray-spotted dog
maybe rubbed. And the mouth of this gray-spotted dog shows
the milk. It peers back and forth, looking up. And tied abut it
is the sleepy-looking dog, like it is lying down calm from a nap,
like a dog that is thinking there is nothing much on. Or perhaps I am wrong about the sleepy-looking dog.

Then the black-standing dog snatches air in its chops, and
a slaver of milk strands the air.

Air claps a slamming of sound—we are as if some lightning
jumped a limb into the barn.

Momma calls us from the porch, says, "What's going on
yonder?

"You all come wash up!" Momma says.

I put the blue velvet sack on my tabletop, and sit down
across from Jeab. It is raining outside by the streetlight's
bloom, in city-blown gustings of rain. "It could use a pin, I
think," I say.

Jeab and me in my kitchen, alone, my window and the rain.

Jeab pulls out my pistol by its grip and holds it flat across
my tabletop. "Used to fuck our 4-H calf," he says. "The shit
we did back then."

I sip my beer and look at him. "You did what?" is what I say.

Outside in the night, egged-in under the moon-monster snake of the blackened trees which line the fence a-round our farm, cattle lie, still and breathing, whitely egg shapes, pale white as breasts, or as stones butted of a graveyard in the dark on this cold March ground. My toes are ice cubes in my shoes. The black of trees across the lighter dark where night is looms. Alive-looking, like in a book of monsters. Some cloud-large snake, with all the cows inside, turns may-be, hisses, sucks up all there is around our farm. And I am swallowed in the night.

Out by a block of almost unseeably dark cow, she looms, pale as wash on a line at night. I move in under the fence-line trees, and smell—sauced-in, on tines of cold—her cow-ma-nure smell, and something else, burst or cut or soured weed cuttings, oak, acorn, old milk—the straw and cow-manure smell of cow, cows outside on the grassless sandlot, bedded down in dark. This is where, and how, Darling is. Look.

Darling turns into, slowly, a papier-mâché cow shape in the night-curtaining, cool, blue-white as milk, as still and as patient as sheep. Now she is, vividly, her horns, her pointed-down bone-wedge head, white-shanked legs, her huge night coloring. Darling moos.

Darling follows along behind me with her nose in her feed bucket, and pushes it into my butt. It is all of a murk of the path to the barn, the small, starred lights of our house growing large and then shattering in saucers of light. Look at it, and blink. Darling lifts her head up from her feed bucket and noses at my arm, like a boxer rubs sweat from a glove. I slap Darling's horn.

"Whoa now, girl," I say to her, and head her to the stall.

We stop at a block of hay in the corral behind the barn, and I snap Darling's lead onto her halter ring. She nods back with her chin the way she does, an act like she is resisting just a little, like at first. My end of the lead around a post. I pat Darling's wither cup, and feel her hide twitch on my palm, weirdly sprung, hide electric as a horse at shying bugs. She doesn't want the lead snapped on. I spread out and fluff some hay for us inside her stall, covering the stall muck of this morning with a rough and thickly haying blanket. Shots of flies skit in the flashlight air. Cloud-thick. I shake feed in Darling's trough and lead her in. Close the gate behind on us.

Sour of piss, and rotted peach. I huff dust up in the air, and bits of hay shreddeds toss and loft afloat about her stall.

It smells. A taste of vinegar or collard.

I have the flashlight on the nail. Underfoot, a rotted rat, or guts, or a pound of burger squishing, everywhere manure in the straw. I get set, and tie her lead in through her feed trough, leg my stool up close to Darling at her ilium, where it dents.

"Come on, get your leg up, girl."

Darling munches. At her feed again.

—This is how you milk a cow.

Head in. With a rhythm of Indian canoes, slow . . . enormous heron birds, teal-blue and winging off a flat lake's water. Elbows lower than your knees, pressing the all of me, until Darling, letting loose her milk, presses the bulk of the barrelous, swollen all of her back at me; we are a balancing act.

I sort of turn it in my hand, like this, like so. One, and then another one, like I am.

Just her milk, my breath. Like so.

—Like this is all the world, inside our barn, the flashlight dark strawed on the boards along the stall walls. And Darling moos.

The warm from pushing her—my head caps leatherly in her ilium where it dents—the warm spots on my knees dug in her flank and in her bloat and punchball stomach. Hear the waters run in Darling's guts like my brother's stomach does when he is going at his weights, or at our TV on the floor. I watch Darling's milk strand in my bucket, streaks of milk which spritz the tin and make the sound of when I milk. And the milk is rising foamed like Daddy's shaving cream will do—or like the milk that clabbers sweet in whipping cream.

And I am lost inside the white.

I close my eyes in floating, darkly in the milk. My soul goes out, and bone pulls from my lost-in-working arms. I am light-less in the deep up in the milk.

I see nakeds squirming, every girl I know, up in the clouds; I get a hard and think of God. Me and God up in the clouds. I have to stop and beat off, do a bit—my sunned and little pocket frog.

Hook my half-full bucket on the nail. My mother, and my fatted aunts, some teachers, and some girls at school, the Stoke girl on the bus, her breasts bared on the straw with me—on Momma and Daddy's turned-down bed, there in their room. The cottoned-white of pillows at the head, and Daddy's smell and sense of him about the room, haunting it, *the stuff of his.* Him!

Darling hums a deeply moo; she moos, and in her head, and in her chest a buzz, a tinnish, stretched-on-cowskin record sound. Then this is all there is, here in the stall, this is all of what there is, and I am in it. Here, the scruffed and knotty boards along the stall, two-by-fours and tin along the roof. And straw and devil's breath around my neck. The devil's breath, it lights and winks in bits of lint, and dust-nothings yellowed in the flashlight's shine done in the stall. I taste of tooth and morning breath, stale inside my mouth. I stop, zip up my pants, quit it.

Us in the night.

In the stall.

I get up, unhook my bucket from the nail. Set it on the bucket stand, and milk.

And Darling kicks.

"Whoa now, girl," I say to her. And milk. Brunt my shoulder on her quarter ham, and push. Darling's leg springs back to where it should. A foot of leg sinks underwater in the straw. I milk some more. I pat Darling's rump and tell her, "Good old girl. This is how to do it."

Good, and warm, and all of what there is, me and my cow.

Darling in our stall of the whole world *in my mind* on our farm.

Our house sounds-in to Darling's stall. I feature Momma with her pots up at the stove. Momma's hair wasped-up and stainy red, but red and also coppering, my momma in her work outfit and nylons on her legs. I stop and put my bucket up, unsnap the lead from Darling's halter ring, and go and let in Darling's calf.

And Darling's calf is like a puppy, or a small dog, more than he is like a bull. He lunges in a challengy and puppy-headed way to me, through dust swarms in the flashlight's shine. I can tell the calf is happy seeing me; he's lonesome-dumb caught in the light, and also sort of sweet-looking. His little pudden-pies of turd. He plays like he's a bigger bull, shovels hooves of dirt, which lift, then clod into the night. Darling's calf, he scratches, looks, sees if I am watching him.

Let him in to Darling.

Watch. Watch him suck.

Darling forward-butts herself and serves her quarters to her calf. She gives in to him and spreads, and stretches once-as-long her neck. She chews her cud. Gnaws it, Darling does. Darling's puppy of a calf butts Darling's bag, bumps his nose amongst the dark bogged under Darling. And I swear I hear some water-something dollop up in Darling . . . watch the froth foam on his mouth sucked to her bag. *It in his mouth,* the bubblings of the milk. His whiskers like a cat. His lips.

Sucking, getting sucked. I turn the flashlight off on us and swallow into dark.

This is what it is amongst the dark, *him in doing her like this.* Darling's calf nosed under Darling in the light slits from the windows of our house. His gibby, bladdered eyes shoved in the light. He butts his head bone in her bag like he is *eating her from out of her,* and God supposed to know it—planned it, anyhow. Darling's calf's legs buttressed bracing him, and spread out like a tent to get a hold, one in his mouth. One aslung with milky drool, bubbles of the milk hung in his spittle. Something more it is, I say, is Darling's calf at doing this. I don't know. Maybe it is less than what it seems. Maybe it is not a lot. I have seen him suck a zillion times . . . I want to take his bitty windpipe here and choke the little fucking shit.

Outside, in the cooler night star widening out our stall, Darling looms. Tuckered crickings in her bones as Darling lolls on through the gate on to the end of our corral, then we loll into our even brighter field out in the dark. Color has some dull in shade on things, in brushings paled. Withered leaf of weed, and rind of sneaker. Darling broadly mottled, black and white. I smack my palm across her rump. There is Daddy's truck hulked in our yard, behind our house. Every light is on inside our house like company inside, or a party going on, grownups cutting up with us. Or just is Jeab. My brother won't turn off a light. Jeab says it isn't squat to him. Leaves them on. My brother at my table with my gun is how Jeab is.

Jeab before. Jeab of now, and with his grin.

Take my cow into the night is how I am when I'm with Darling. "Come on, girl," I say to her. "Come on, girl. Come on."

Darling plods the winter weed caught in the lamplight from our house that draws manila on our yard and gauzes fainter to the barn, and darkens then to nothing-tugs and stringy slips of light across our field. I look back, but I don't know if there is light on me, or just is in my eyes. I can't tell.

Some weed runs dark half up my leg. Look to her to know if we're in light.

Darling looming in the dark.
Jeab and my gun.

Look!
Look at Darling, whitely, and in black done in the night!
"Come on, girl," I say to her. And I head Darling to the fence-line trees, snaked-in in the night.
"Come on, love," I say. **Q**

Thinking About Momma

When Momma dies, I am going to have her stuffed by this friend of mine, George, who did the rabbit you can see over there on the mantel. George kept the rabbit pretty much the same—I can show you pictures later if you want to see them. The only difference is George putting the rabbit on the wide stick for some reason, something like he had extra sticks about, and pulling back the sides of the rabbit's mouth, so, George said, the rabbit would look like the type of rabbit she was, the type that growled and thumped that back foot—see how it is raised off of the stick?—whenever George showed up to sit in or take me out.

I did not complain.

I had given George free rein over the rabbit; but Momma, now Momma is a different story.

Already warned him about her. Told George exactly how I want Momma done, which is the way I think she would want to have herself done if she knew anything about this.

First, the hair.

Momma sure loves hair.

Give Momma the touches of raspberry and peach she said she always wanted, no matter if you have to use latex on her—who's going to know, anyhow?—and sweep her hair way up, all curled and glazed over, looking wet under the overhead lights and as perfect as can be, the way Momma liked it before the operation made her all cheeks and chins, making Momma say that no matter how higher than high that queer down the road piled her hair up, she could never look the way she did before the operation, more hair than face, like some sort of animal.

George told me not to worry; he says by adding pieces of hair dyed Momma's color he will make her hair any size that is necessary. Even trim Momma's face, if that is what I want to have done to her.

Which is not a bad idea. Except for Momma never wanting to get a face fix, always saying how she thought those women with fixed faces looked like they were wearing masks that were able to be torn off their faces if you got your fingernails just right there at the edges of their eyes and pulled.

Momma said when the time comes for things to wrinkle and to sag, let them, and thank God you do not have to worry about it happening anymore. It is a blessing for a woman to grow old, Momma said.

Not that I think you can take Momma's word for it, because Momma has one of those faces that, even now with her cheeks and chins, never looks as old as it is. The giveaway, I think, is Momma's eyebrows. Shaved them off over and over in her day, for style—so many times they finally stopped growing in—and she has to pencil them in, in thin brown lines.

The other giveaway is Momma's body, which used to be a body that could squeeze between parked cars, before they carved such a chunk out of Momma. Oh, how Momma cannot but not stop feeling that maybe she is not much anymore!

Maybe if they had brought it to her as she lay in the white light, no eyebrows, her hair squashed and dumped into her face, so that she kept squeezing strands of it and saying to me, "It's a mess, isn't it?" Maybe if they had brought it to her the way they had brought me to her, and then let Momma take it in both hands as she once took me in both hands, feeling its weight, the weight now lifted off her body. Maybe if they had let Momma turn it over in her hands, maybe even look through some magnifying glass at the stuff that made them have to take it off of her, maybe then Momma could have understood and parted with it, feeling a lightness, a freshness, of body. Or maybe if they had let Momma take it home with her, in a jar of some kind of chemical, the jar itself in a brown bag, like the ones Momma used to sign my name to and fold over the top, the way, she said, the dentist had let her take her wisdom teeth, her carrying them home, dried bloody and color of sand, in a plastic bag knotted over and in on itself, and once home, then Momma could have put the brown bag with the plastic bag in the sequined box Poppa gave Momma before he left forever.

Enough Poppa.

Even if Poppa comes back, I am not going to get George to stuff him the way George stuffed the rabbit and the way George is going to stuff Momma.

George will tuck in that stomach of hers, having grown to such a size Momma said hugging me makes the back of her arms hurt. And George will cut out her kneecaps, too—making it necessary, he says, for me to take Momma out of those dragging-along skirts she wears and ruffles up—turns and ruffles up if George is in the room, watching her or not—to the top cuff of her white socks not able to be seen through even when wet but which Momma swears make her feet look smaller than they really are and that Momma insists on wearing each day, even now with the weather turning warm. And then George will cut along the insides of Momma's upper legs, which, Momma says, rub together whenever she walks, making her wonder if it is worth her walking at all. She wonders how it would be to run upstairs, two at a time again, the way she hears George and me run up whenever we come over and have to go up the stairs to where Momma is in pillows, pushing buttons, or already on the phone with her only friend in this whole wide world.

Lurriece.

Who also has, according to George, the only legs he has ever seen that deserve to be framed and hung on the wall across from his bed. But no offense intended to mine, George says.

None taken, I told him, just so long as you promise to shape Momma a pair of legs better than Lurriece's.

George says he will go one better, that after shaving Momma's legs himself he will work as long as he has to to shape Momma a pair of legs God will wish He had made for her Himself, and then George will personally buy and pull on Momma a pair of panty hose, with rhinestones encircling the ankles, panty hose so soft that God will not be able to resist reaching down and feeling up Momma's legs, then feeling up farther than that, and God feeling Himself so all excited that He ends up doing it with Momma, right there, however God does it, right through her panty hose, George bet. Can you imagine that? George asked. Can you imagine God doing it with your momma?

I told George no, not me, and not to touch Momma's backside or hips, because of those nights when claims of nightmares brought me to Momma's bedside, my backside against hers rising up over mine, mine pressing, sometimes rubbing, Momma finally turning over and putting an arm over me, as if we were lovers.

As for the top of Momma, George cannot touch the top of Momma either, what after her refusing to have another one put in and her locking the bathroom door on me, who always used to go to the bathroom as she sponged along her body, but who now goes to the bathroom looking into a bathtub without Momma, and now with Momma sponging, with me talking to her from the other side of the door.

George cannot even look at Momma without her being hooked up in back, because the way Momma tells it, it makes me feel that she thinks too many people have looked at her already without her being hooked up in back. Besides, Momma and me, we have discussed things, sort of made a pact of how when she knows soon is the time, I get in—next to her or on top of her—it is up to me, Momma said—and unhook her. Lifting her arm up, I am going to stick my nose under, smelling all there is of Momma, kissing her from where the two thick bands come down and get joined up by other thin bands going back and forth between, looking, Momma says, like a track for trains, only bumped with bumps which were supposed to, but never did, flatten out. I am going to kiss all those bumps on the track that shoots across to almost the other one, but then curls on itself instead and ends right there over Momma's heart in the biggest bump of them all, a bump that makes Momma feel, she says, as if she is one of those animals Poppa and Lurriece's Jared used to bring home hanging from ropes after a day on the lands, to slice clean for a supper that Momma refused to eat.

Momma asked me not to kiss the bump. But before I lay my ear—dangles on, as Momma wants to feel the cold pinch on where she used to be—right over her heart—I am taking the bump between my lips no matter what Momma says, and I am staying on Momma, with every beat of Momma, smelling and kissing and touching the other one, until I do not hear anything out of Momma anymore.

After that, Momma says, the body is all mine to do with whatever I want to, except not to put it into a coffin and shove it into the stone wall of the stone place where Poppa bought space for both of them before he left forever.

I can burn it, Momma says, and keep it in the sequined box, and have my daughter do the same to me.

I am telling Momma not to worry.

George and I will take care of her. George and I will make all the arrangements for her. Fact is, with whatever Momma leaves me, I am going to give Momma what she told me, as I was growing up, she had off in some corner of the house, this room she had roped off from the rest of the house with thick red ropes, which were twisted together but which were invisible, just like the room behind the ropes, this room of Momma's, this room of all gold—gold ceiling crossed with gold beams, painted with gold flowers that when Momma steps onto the gold carpet, filled with gold lions having the faces of gold dogs, the gold flowers drop from the gold ceiling and rotate, with Momma unfolding herself on the gold sofa, with Momma hearing the air shaking through the gold curtains tied with gold bows, with Momma gazing into the gold fountain of a gold girl holding a gold rabbit, spouting gold water that turns Momma's hands and mouth gold whenever she kneels on the gold carpet and cups the gold water into her thirsty mouth.

How George and I would make such a fountain, or find one, we have no idea. But we figure the fountain can go by the wayside so long as the rest of the room is right for the way Momma sees it, us putting Momma where she says the fountain is supposed to go, us putting Momma standing in a glass case, edged in gold, which George offered to make for her himself. George said he would also hang the overhead lights and the mirrors, edged in gold, if they are really what I want and if I can afford getting them up on the wall behind Momma and on the wall across from Momma, so that Momma looks like she is going on and on forever.

Will you also seal off the entrance to the room with glass, I asked George, and make Momma mechanized, so that Momma can walk around her room, putting her hands up to her hair as if she is fixing it off her face, and sit on her gold sofa, with her lips going right in sync with this tape I am going to make Momma make?

George says he's no mechanic, and if I want Momma to move and to talk, I had just better go and get myself another boy.

Then George brought in Lurriece, telling me that we should get Lurriece in on it, since Momma has always liked the way Lurriece does rooms, and, who knows, Lurriece might be able to find the fountain, if not exact, then something close enough, in one of the shops she goes to to find things for her own shop, and all George would have to do then is to mix water and gold paint and get it running through the fountain, which, George says, he might could see his way clear to trying.

No mechanic for me, thanks!

And Lurriece is not going to find out about Momma until

Momma is ready for her to. If something is said to Lurriece sooner, Lurriece might not like the idea and might go to telling Momma, who, in turn, might ask us not to do what George and I have been planning to do all along. But Lurriece sure would be someone to talk over clothes with, though. Because, except for the panty hose George is going to buy—which means Momma has to be in some sort of skirt, I suppose—I admit that I do not know how to dress Momma, and George sure will not talk clothes with me. Nothing Momma has is small enough for whatever size George will end up making her. So I will have to buy or sew Momma something. But what color should the something be?

Momma's best is blue. But if George gives her the touches of raspberry and peach in her hair that Momma says she has always wanted, then Momma ought to be in something pink or peach, so that what she has on goes with her hair. But Momma does not wear pink anywhere else but on her nails, and she does not wear peach anywhere else but on her lips, so what choice do I have but to paint Momma's nails pink? Momma's lips peach? And to sew her something gold. Which will go with the pink nails, the peach lips, and the gold room.

And the something gold I am going to make will be full on the top, slim over the hips, and slit up the sides, so that your eyes will follow down to the sparkle of Momma's ankles and to the sparkle of her shoes, since I am going to have George shave off the sides of Momma's feet and the backs of her heels, even cut off a few toes—which I will probably keep for the sequined box—I mean, if I need to make her feet even smaller to get them into the shoes.

Then there is this hat I was thinking of making for Momma—a high hat, hollow in the center, which would fit Momma the way a crown fits a queen: up on top, in the midst of her hair, as if growing out of the hair itself, yet kind of pushed forward, as if the hat might topple off if Momma bent her head down to look at her sparkles down below. The high hollow hat would be made out of some kind of animal fur, something plain like rabbit, I suppose, that could be dyed gold, and filled here and there with some of the extra eyes George has from the animals he has found out on the road and has not been able to fix up enough to sell.

So that is how I see Momma: as a queen, standing in her glass box edged around the edges in gold, roped off by red ropes from the rest of the house.

Only problem is, I do not know how George should have Momma standing. Maybe facing front, her hands behind her, resting fists down on her hips; maybe with one leg and shoulder coming forward, the other leg and shoulder staying back, and Momma looking over the shoulder coming forward as if she is stepping right on through the glass; and maybe with one leg straight, the other bent, with the toe of the shoe down but the heel up, and Momma turning her waist and shoulders and head toward the bent leg, with her arms hanging at her sides.

George says he will sketch these and more, and let me take a look at all of them before he explains to me why, in his professional opinion, there is only one way for Momma to stand—with her feet a little apart, with her hands on her hips, one hip a little forward, chin up, but not too much—so that when you stand on the other side of the glass your eyes meet Momma's eyes.

As for the expression of her eyes and face, I am going to let them look just the way they look by the time George shows up with the bag he plans to wrap her in and put her in in the back of his van for the ride over to his place. George flat refuses to take a hammer to Momma's jaw. He says if he peels back Momma's skin to where her hair starts, messes with some of the bones underneath, and then rolls the skin forward again, there is the chance that no matter how careful he is that Momma will end up having reddish-blackish-bluish blotches, which only makeup of a color much darker than Momma's own skin color could ever cover over, giving Momma a tan she never had or seemed to want to have during those summers we spent with Lurriece and Lurriece's Jared at their stinking beachhouse.

But thinking about Momma not wanting to get a tan gets me to thinking about how Momma might not want to get all dressed up to stand in a box—under lights, in a room roped off from the rest of the house, either. That Momma might just want to be Momma—skirted and socked and lopsided, all cheeks and chins.

But then I think George must be right—I should talk to Lurriece before I plan anything else. Talk to Lurriece about having George put Momma in here, right over there, under the mantel, a good ways down from the rabbit—so that when you walk into the room you do not see one and not the other. Maybe I should talk to Lurriece about having George sit Momma down in a chair with her white socks on, with her skirt folded up into itself, with her arms just hanging, as if without strength, so that her hands lie wide open on her skirt, her face, without anything on it, just sagging, and her eyes sort of saying—as you kneel before her and look into them—that there is nothing else which needs to be said about what has happened and will never happen again, so help me God. **Q**

The Tenants

"If they don't like it, they can leave," the mother said to the daughter. They were sitting in the TV room on the middle floor.

The TV room was the biggest room in the house. The room was so big that if you were sitting in one corner and you wanted to talk to someone sitting in another corner you had to shout. The TV sat on a wood stand in the middle of the room. A daybed and three big chairs occupied the room's corners.

"No one's going to burn up my house," the mother said to the daughter. "If they think I'm going to sit here and let them burn up my house, they're crazy."

The daughter nodded.

"He's the one's that's crazy," the mother said. "He sits around all day long doing nothing."

The daughter nodded again.

The daughter sat up very straight in her chair. She wore a blue dress with a white collar, simple blue shoes, and white stockings. The daughter worked for a bank part-time.

The mother sat home all day long and did nothing.

The mother said, "A grown man like that getting money from the city. People like that shouldn't be getting money from the city. People like that are lazy."

"He could get work if he wanted to," the daughter said.

The mother said, "Now take me, I'm old and sick. But that doesn't matter. The city won't give me anything." The mother said, "No wonder his family wanted to get rid of him."

The daughter said, "She told me that her family didn't want her, either."

"All I know is that they're not going to set this house on fire, not as long as I own it," the mother said. "As far as that goes, they'll cook on a hot plate for as long as they live here. If they don't like it, they can find another place. They can leave tomorrow, for all I care."

The mother lay on the daybed in a flowered housedress. She had a kerchief the same color as the housedress tied backwards on her head.

"Why did you do that?" the daughter said.

"Why did I do what?"

"Why do you have that kerchief tied backwards on your head like that?" the daughter said.

"That's the way it was made," the mother answered.

"What do you mean, that's the way it was made? I've never seen that done before," the daughter said, "and I've seen everything."

"The knot was already tied in, so you just slip it on your head this way. See? Look here," the mother said.

The mother took the kerchief off her head.

The daughter looked.

The mother put the kerchief back on her head. The mother said, "Any minute now she'll be down here standing in the door with a plate of steaming hot food in her hand. She always asks me if she can sit down. What does she think I'm going to do, make her stand?"

"You should have seen her the other day," the daughter said. "She had on a pair of big blue pants, an oversized red shirt, and a pair of dirty white sneakers that also did not fit."

"Where were the other two?" the mother asked.

The mother and the daughter never called the tenants by their names. They called them him or her or the other two or the other one or the little one or the baby, whichever they thought fit the best when they were saying it.

"She said he was upstairs trying to get the baby to go to sleep because the baby was fretting."

"That baby is always fretting," the mother said to the daughter. "All that baby does all day long is fret. You'd think there was something wrong with that baby."

"There has to be something wrong with that baby," the daughter said. "Look at that baby's mother and father."

"She's always talking," the mother said. "Even if you don't ask her anything, she'll tell you something anyway. She can't come in here and sit quiet and watch TV like us. Oh no, she always has to come in and tell you something."

"She told me that after he put the baby to sleep he was going to go downtown to see about a job in a big office."

The mother just looked at the daughter.

"Now you tell me who in the world would give him work in a big office," the daughter said to the mother.

"What would he do?" the mother said.

The daughter said she wasn't quite sure, but whatever it was, he'd have to wear a suit. "He said if he gets this job, his office will have a view of the whole city."

"Oh! She said she's seen this done before," the mother said to the daughter.

"She's seen what done before?"

"The kerchief with the knot in the front."

The daughter waved her hand. "She hasn't seen any-thing," the daughter said. "She's just saying that."

The mother said, "But she told me where I got it from. She said . . ."

"He must not have been able to get that baby to sleep, because right after she came down he came down and sat the baby next to her. He told her he was going out looking. When I said, 'Here we go again,' he got mad," the daughter said.

The mother said, "What did he say?"

"He said, 'I pay my way.' "

"And what did you say?"

"I said, 'The city pays your way.' Then he had the nerve to tell me that if he got this job he'd be able to pay for the whole house. He'd buy the whole house out from underneath us. He said this would be his house and he'd put us upstairs with no gas."

The mother laughed. The mother said, "The other day

she had the nerve to get smart. I had to sit up and make sure it was her standing there and not somebody who had walked in off the street while I was sleeping."

The daughter said, "Let her get smart with me, I'll put her in her place."

"Shush," the mother said. "I think I hear something."

They heard footsteps coming down the stairs.

The woman tenant came rushing in and stood in the far corner of the room with the baby on her hip and with a plate of steaming hot food in her hand. "At work," the woman tenant shouted before the mother could ask where "he" was. "And his name is Jessie," the woman tenant said. "And my name is Lila. And his name is Jessie Junior. Jessie Junior is what we call the baby."

The woman tenant had on clothes that fit for a change.

"Those are our names," the woman tenant said. "Not her, not him, not the other one, not the other two, not no little one or anything like that!"

Then the woman tenant turned to the daughter. "And that goes for you, too!" the woman tenant said, and sat down with the baby and started eating. **Q**

The Stories

[1]

I began watching the stories again because well for one thing we have a decent TV now color and a nice den and I just sit back in Dick's La-Z-Boy and everything is so real-looking and also because our next-door neighbor Mary Jane is a clerk in Johnny's school and she takes him home I don't have to drive the seven-tenths of a mile to get him the school bus won't because it's under a mile. I didn't think I'd like living here I told Dick no we don't have the money and he said I'm on rung 2 of the ladder and it's a new house we'll be the first to live in it don't you understand the first he said you're afraid sweetheart but don't be you'll see how much better for Johnny too they'll stop picking on him and we chose the house I was so nervous so nervous I never told Dick I thought I would throw up on that nice floor that wasn't even carpeted yet that smell of yellow pine that's why Dick said it was so sweet it was so new it was going to be ours. I never had a virgin but Dick had me so I knew what he meant now by taking off the wrapper that's why I was so nervous I remembered all those jokes the men made at our wedding. We would have our own yard already fenced in with chain-link fence and our garage in the basement and the houses didn't seem as close as they were really because the way the streets curve it's not like they're looking over one another's shoulder and the trees are little babies with little collars or little fences and they'll get big someday.

After we moved in I was still so nervous and all the carpeting wasn't in and the drywall cracked in the hallway and the concrete crumbled in the driveway but it was all covered in the contract and Dick called and the men came and actually did fix everything. I felt so good about living here I began wearing makeup and Dick said see I knew you'd like it and sometimes when I went shopping and saw a blouse or an outfit I liked and wasn't sure about spending the money Dick would tell me to buy it. Remember I'm on rung 2 that was our little joke.

Little by little the new furniture came a den whoever had a den except on TV. Dick said if nothing else we wouldn't have nicer neighbors and we were hardly moved in when we had dinner with Mary Jane and John and Mary Jane said I'll be happy to take Johnny to and from school if he doesn't mind what with the price of gas. And on the other side there's Kathy and Bill and we didn't get to know them until later Bill works shiftwork not that he's doing day work he's a supervisor but he's still on shift and they're real nice too and have a little baby girl and sometimes Kathy asks me to watch the baby or sometimes we go out together and in the afternoon if I watch her while the stories are on it's okay because that little girl sleeps with her bottle so quiet you get up to make sure she's still breathing but otherwise you forget she's there.

In my favorite story Beth is thinking about getting a job to keep up with inflation you know and it just so happens that their next-door neighbor Tom has an opening in his insurance company she hasn't worked in years but everyone gives her their blessings and off she goes and one day she is staying late she's still new on the job and she's conscientious and wants to do a good job and she stays half an hour or more late and is packing up her things to leave when *oops* she's scared half to death because Tom is still in his office and he comes out.

I'm so sorry, he says.

Oh, she says trying to catch her breath it takes her a long time. I didn't know you were still here.

It takes him a long time to smile he's looking at her so hard. Bosses work late too, he says. And *I* knew *you* were here. I don't like the way he says that but he's such a nice guy and it's funny the way she's looking at him. Then he smiles back.

The scene changes to this mean person of a mother-in-law who's secretly in love with her son (the mother is) but she's so ugly I go to the laundry room and check my detergent and then they cut to the fourteen-year-old girl who tried for months to buy a gun and now she's got it she's going to kill the first woman her father ever really loved. I scoot back in I can't believe that little girl will actually do it and what's going to happen to Tom and Beth? There's still time in the program there's another commercial it's in the supermarket just like the other day with Kathy and the baby and then Tom and Beth are smiling at each other again and Tom says very innocently I'm going straight home I'll drive you and Beth says I'm still so surprised you're here the keys are still in my hand I was going to lock up. She drops the keys and stoops and his hand closes over hers and the music starts with the titles.

Johnny came home later with a black eye. Mary Jane came in with him to explain and didn't like the way I looked at her and she gave me a look back but then laughed. He's still the new kid in town you know they'll try to get him in trouble before he becomes one of the crowd you know pick on him and I said what did they say you did and he said this fat bully said Johnny stole his pen. Johnny's always real quiet reading books and nobody knows that he's off in his room with library books and I thought Dick would know what to say to him Mary Jane said a lot of the kids here were new a lot of them didn't know each other and it was just hard for them to make friends and I told Johnny he could go out and play if his eye didn't hurt too bad but he went to his room. Mary Jane said he'll work it out he's a good kid kids are so cruel to one another constantly challenging teasing hurting one another so mean I remember when I was a kid we teased and played jokes and all but I don't remember us ever being so mean. You should see what happens in that school some of the things they bring kids to the office for nice kids regular homes not the bused ones.

This was the first time I noticed how nice Mary Jane was dressed for work really nice not like our old neighborhood where people slopped on any old thing over here they have respect for other people so I was glad I was wearing makeup and dressing better and I could sense that she was looking me over too and we both felt good about one another and I asked her to sit down for a cup of coffee and she said she wished she could rest her weary buns but you know how it is when you work there's a million things to do when you get home. When she left Johnny still hadn't come out of his room so I went up and said let me see and it didn't look so bad and he said Mommy it really hurts and gave me such a look that I said okay I won't force you to go outside if you don't want to.

Johnny was all anxious about his father coming home like he wanted to tell him what happened and when Dick came home they went down to the den they weren't there very long I was making dinner and Dick came up alone and said everything was all right that on Saturday he was buying a punching bag and hanging it in the utility room and I said Dick the boy's just barely nine and Dick said he's going to have to learn to use his hands defend himself better and I said what does Johnny think and Dick said he didn't know he's never hit one and I said well what about the fight he was in and Dick said they're picking on him again even here that's why the punching bag maybe after he learns to use it they won't pick on him and I said Mary Jane says all the kids are hard on one another and they're just picking on him till they get to know him. But that's hard Dick said cause he's so quiet we can't teach him how to talk but we can teach him how to fight Mary Jane didn't know him before. He went to the other school long enough to make friends and didn't because they never stopped picking on him where is he I said I want to see how his eye's doing and Dick said he went out to the library on his bike.

Out on his bike? Dinner's almost ready what about his eye he told me it hurt?

He told me his eye didn't hurt he just had some books to return.

I sighed and Dick came up from behind and cupped his

hands on my breasts and kissed my neck it felt good I said stop don't give me a hickie maybe later and he went to change and then Johnny came home just before dinner perfect timing I said wash up let me see your eye first and he came over and I looked and said looks okay you have a good talk with your dad? Okay he said he's buying me a punching bag I know I said and Johnny turned and scooted off to the bathroom.

Next day the car broke down at the shopping center right after we had lunch too which was a drag with Kathy and the baby we were all done and the car wouldn't start and a man came over and said it's flooded but I never flooded a motor before there's always a first time he said and after a few minutes it still wouldn't start and another man came by with jumper cables but as soon as he heard the car he said it wasn't the battery but a resistor and I'd have to call a garage. All I'd ever had before was flat tires and dead batteries not breakdowns so I called a garage which was less than a mile away and the man said lady the wrecker's out but we'll radio him over. We waited it shouldn't have been more than fifteen minutes then it was half an hour and I began to get mad then forty-five minutes and I was tired of telling Kathy they were probably out on other calls they probably forgot there's only so much you can do with a nine-month-old baby inside a car waiting for a wrecker so finally I got out and went back inside the mall to find a phone and I said mister I called an hour ago and he said lady remember the fog this morning everybody's left their lights on now they can't start their cars and when I stepped outside there was a man hitching up the wrecker to our car and I looked at my watch and I knew I was going to miss the story today I wanted to see what happened to Beth and Tom I asked Kathy if she watched that one she said no the baby usually napped then and she napped too I told the man it was probably a resistor and he said they'd check it out at the garage and I apologized to Kathy again and she said it's not your fault but I could see how antsy the baby got missing its nap and how tired Kathy was getting and then we had to ride in the cab of the wrecker over to the garage maybe they have a TV there and Kathy tried to make a game of it but the baby fell right to sleep and slept all through the noise at the garage they didn't have a TV they hooked up all kinds of meters and gauges and the man said yup it's a resistor and it took five minutes to fix and only cost five dollars but the towing cost twenty and that night I told Dick it was a little piece of brick with prongs that cost twenty-five bucks I think I should have a new car and before he had the chance to get angry I said look I'm willing to get a part-time job and he started in on that rung 2 business but I said all the promotions and raises you get won't keep up with inflation like what they've been saying on the news and I know it's true and he said you'll have to hire someone to clean and I said I know I thought it all out and he said there are a lot of wives working these days I know a lot of men never would've let their wives work before but it's different now. He's so understanding such a dear and the next morning I went out with the paper and started applying and they said they'd call back and I figured it was the brush-off they already had people picked out but I was surprised how many jobs were advertised and most of them weren't taken when I got there. When I got home I had time to catch my story I'd only missed the very beginning and as soon as the picture comes in Beth and Tom are dining in a fancy restaurant holding hands Beth is looking at the gravel as they walk to his car in the meanwhile the old witch pours rat poison in her daughter-in-law's wine and Olivia the young girl with the gun loads it and plans to pull it on her father's sweetheart at dinner she rehearses her speech she's such a beautiful girl Olivia how did she get so crazy? Is she in love with her father like the old witch loves her son these things happen all the time her father's sweetheart is so nice I hope she doesn't get hurt maybe Olivia will just wing her or something.

Tom holds the door open for Beth I can't remember the last time Dick did that for me and then he gets in and she says it was a lovely evening she looks at her wedding band soft music is playing in the restaurant and he says I never thought I'd ever feel this way about someone twenty years ago yes but not now he reaches for her and she accepts and the camera closes in on their faces their mouths open. My God these actors' tongues flash into each other's mouths and it takes my breath away my whole body throbs it's not a fake what do their husbands and wives or whomever think it's such a long kiss they're still kissing. That night I played a little game with Dick I had to tell him about it I said they were really kissing and he said how do they usually kiss and I showed him how their mouths aim for each other and veer off at the last second or sometimes they keep their lips real tight and he kisses her upper lip and she his lower lip but not really kissing I showed him what they did that day and I kept my tongue soft and full and plunged it into his mouth and though it got him all excited and was okay for me too it wasn't like the surprise when I saw it on TV.

I took a job at the bank instead of the tire shop near the mall and the first day I'm on my own window and John Mary Jane's husband walked in and said I'm very disappointed you didn't take the job with us and I never even realized that's the tire shop where he's manager he said I didn't want you to think I was pulling strings for you but the others thought you could handle it it's quieter here though there's no way you can escape all the banging in the bays back there. He asked me out for a cup of coffee or something stronger to celebrate my job and I said thanks but I wanted to be home when Johnny got home from school I didn't want the idea of me working to be a shock how's he doing John said it's hard to know I said but Dick got him a punching bag and he hasn't gotten in trouble lately but you should know this from M.J. that's what he called her. He looked at his watch and said see you later neighbor which was good timing because we were getting our last rush before the bank closed.

I was missing the stories and asked around among the girls

if anyone knew what was happening on my favorite one and a girl chimes in Beth's husband hasn't found out yet but Tom's wife is going to tell him and the drinks got switched the old hag poisoned herself instead she's in the hospital repenting before she dies Olivia's gun didn't go off she didn't know it had a safety how do you know all this I said. I watch them she said and it turned out there were two shifts of four hours each she had the early one I didn't know they had part-timers on in the morning so I went to Mr. Snyder and asked him and he didn't even ask why just said if I could find someone to switch but it couldn't be permanent because they wanted everyone to get to know as many customers as possible at the window and I said that would be fine and had no trouble switching and left for work not long after Johnny left with Mary Jane and got home in plenty of time to flip on the TV I can set my hair while it's on you know. I wasn't working mornings very long when John came back in like he's surprised I'm there he's come for the day's cash I get the feeling someone else really counts it out for him I'm flattering myself but I felt a little shiver up my spine imagining things he seemed absentminded it couldn't be an act and while I counted out the tens he asked me to lunch I lost my place and gave him a dirty look and started over again meanwhile picturing the pain and suffering on TV and think-ing I don't need that because Beth's husband is going crazy he loves her so much how could she do this to him she seems so innocent she's never thought about him in that way it made me nervous and after I finished counting there's no one behind him he said this is an innocent request we're business associ-ates. I laughed and he said 11:45 and the whole rest of the morning I knew it wasn't okay because I'd made plans to lunch where I needed to shop and so I was very nervous and angry at John when we met he drove to a fancy place across town I didn't want to go so far I told him I asked if Mary Jane liked this place he said don't tell her she might misunderstand I said misunderstand what? If Dick showed up at the school and said hey I'm in the neighborhood let's go to lunch I'd take it at face value what more is there? None he said but I didn't know M.J. and then he changed the subject and asked if I would tell Dick and I said of course. The waitress came and we ordered drinks I never drank with lunch in my life why shouldn't I tell him he's my husband he tells me everything and as soon as I said that I knew the look John was going to give me and he did. How did I really know how Dick spent the day but I trust him I said there's no reason to think he's not faithful thank you I said the wine was making me light-headed. But faithful and getting a little on the side aren't the same thing he said. It doesn't mean he doesn't love you it's just the way men are and what about women I said women too he said how about you and I looked away could feel my face all red this bastard made it sound like I invited him.

Then the wine began to burn my stomach the idea Dick was fooling around the way John took it for granted made me feel like a dummy of course he does all men do why didn't I realize it was part of rung 2 or the way these boys get to rung 3 and just while I was thinking that John said it's the way to climb the ladder I thought my private life is just all over the table with bits of ice and water spilled from the glass I felt cut off like a membrane tearing and setting me free loose and unconnected out in space I see Dick and another woman and Johnny in school being picked on and he isn't connected to me either and suddenly I felt very cold and shivered and John moved closer and asked what's wrong and I said the air conditioning and he placed his leg next to mine it was nice to feel the contact in the darkness of the restaurant glass tinkling in the distance soft music too he took my hand your nails are so red this is what they use on the Ping-Pong balls on TV you know the girls with the white suits but he didn't know what I was talking about it doesn't peel.

The hamburgers came they were the biggest I'd ever seen and so juicy there was no neat way to eat them they drip out of your mouth get all over your hands neither of us were hungry I had this fresh glass of wine they have such big glasses

I finished it before we left even though it was making me cold I felt better when I got outside into the hot day. But soon we were in a motel where it was cold again I told him to be kind I didn't know what would happen when he kissed me I could only feel his breath on my cheek he was all excited in a rush I had to keep telling him to slow down and wait for me I'm cold let me warm up and he said okay and then started to wind up like a record playing faster and faster until it's screeching higher than normal and I had to laugh to myself I just couldn't get excited. Then he plunged in and it wasn't funny anymore just hurt it was so unromantic I wanted to throw up the little I ate but he was done quickly and he said maybe it'll be better next time and I said I don't want a next time and he shrugged like suit yourself it doesn't matter he already got the notch on his gun he should have a holster for his penis all notched out he counted the different women not the fucks it was all funny again until I realized this was Mary Jane's husband who was supposed to be our good neighbor and I'd have to joke with him at the barbecue and he drove me back to my car said in passing it's our little secret right it's nothing to lose sleep over right and I nodded but it was all about beat and get beat but I didn't feel dirty or vanquished just cut off without feeling it was not at all like Tom and Beth who felt real passion this was something else. I felt terribly lonely I dreaded those two strangers coming home and calling me Mom and Lover.

[2]

Dick used the punching bag much more than Johnny I could hear him under the kitchen as I made dinner the bag going *ratada-tatada-ratada-tatada* and Johnny was too young to hit it with that kind of steadiness so he just blasted it here and there right jabs and left jabs and watched the bag bounce he did it for Dick he wasn't interested at all in that rhythm business but Dick was telling him how to fight you see this bully comes up to you see and says your mama this and he thinks you're a sissy you're never going to do anything except tell on him which will give him all the more reason to beat up on you so instead of giving him the chance you haul off right there with a left jab that catches him completely off guard and a right hook that knocks him down or into the wall like this *jab-atada-tatada-* KA-BOOM—*atada-tatada* now let me see you do it   again again

In the meanwhile Beth's husband doesn't want to let her go for Tom he still loves her just call it over with call it an affair and she says but I love him and he says but you love me too and she says lov*ed* and he says are you sure we've shared so much you know sometimes love changes but it doesn't die and you could love more than one person at the same time and you feel sorry for him but then you think he might be weird until you realize he's just super-tolerant and doesn't want to lose Beth and she's hurt because she does love him but she loves Tom more and so that's the choice she has to make. So he's hurt you don't know what he's going to do but you know Tom's wife's going crazy at first she was going to sue him for everything but now you think she's going to go insane but maybe Beth's husband will save her. I don't care though things are getting strange and dramatic on that show and I'm not sure I want to keep watching it there's another one on at the same time the girls at the bank are all talking about that's full of gangsters and people actually in bed and people jumping out of windows and dying in fires it's so realistic. I'm thinking the old witch might not die after all maybe she's reformed taught herself a lesson but she's been so rotten can a person that bad ever turn good you spend your whole life hurting people and suddenly you become an angel? But maybe she wasn't sour her whole life maybe they'll flash back to her younger days find out how she got hurt.

Mary Jane calls and says I better get right over to the school Johnny's in trouble I'd just gotten home didn't have time to change just freshened my makeup and got in the car it took two minutes to get there Johnny was in the principal's office staring at his hands the principal said those hands of his are lethal weapons. The principal's very young not an old bald tyrant but a good-looking young man in a three-piece suit and a black mustache and black hair and when he said that about Johnny's hands I wanted to laugh right in his face he was so serious. Does he fight in golden gloves? I can't help smiling he was looking me over at the same time I said golden gloves don't you know anything about any of your students his dad bought him a punching bag he doesn't even know how to use it yet he misses most of the time.

Well he almost broke a boy's nose in the lunchroom the witnesses said he hit Willie with a combination just hauled off and blasted him and the blood flew out of Willie's nose apparently there was no provocation it seemed Johnny was Willie's only friend they were always together though I don't know why Johnny's so serious he could be a psychotic loner. Why did you do it he suddenly shouts at Johnny did you want to break his nose knock an eye loose?

Johnny leaped out of his seat into my arms he never let me alone he stole my lunch stole my lunch money my ice-cream money he said he would kill me slowly break my arm break my leg nobody'd notice I wouldn't dare scream and soon I'd be broke all to pieces so I had to do it Mommy he kept walking in back of me breathing down my neck threatening me.

Why didn't you tell me why didn't you tell your father or Mary Jane or even your principal here?

He said he'd know if I told anyone he had ways of finding out and it would be a lot worse so I had to stop him I wanted to smash his head to pieces on the floor but once he was down he looked so helpless I   I

Where is this boy I said I want to see him.

We think your son needs we're going to recommend him for

I want to see this Willie is he still

He's in the infirmary and a clerk from the office took me over just a few doors and I saw this huge hulk of a boy who seemed too big too old even for the sixth grade his fat face covered with an ice pack it looked like he had breasts you can't talk to him the nurse said I don't want to I said and my heels sounded like firecrackers on my way back to the principal. You mean you're accusing my son of beating up that monster in there?

We know Willie has problems we know his family background but we don't know Johnny his teacher says he reads in class constantly doesn't pay attention just reads we're recommending him for psychiatric evaluation.

Why don't you go sell real estate or life insurance I told him.

You read my mind exactly lady but until then I'm in charge here.

Johnny has always been quiet but he's always been gentle and you don't know your students or what's going on in your school and you think you know something accusing my son of beating up the school bully a boy twice his size and probably age too almost. Calm down lady calm down don't you see if Johnny'd been beaten up it would be a different story. Different story my foot you're blaming the victim for the crime he's not crazy you are with all your half-assed school psychology you think you know what kids do what they think you don't know what it's like going through life being bullied picked on and I took Johnny and we left. He snuggled against me on the front seat and we drove home he was sticking to me in the heat but I didn't mind.

My poor baby why didn't you tell us when it first started we could have done something I didn't want to make trouble he says and I thought where was Mary Jane why didn't she stick up for Johnny is she afraid of that tough-talking snotnose of a principal she knows Johnny reads a lot builds model planes. Suddenly I felt I knew my son again he's part of my flesh drawn back to me from across that emptiness I knew I could protect him take care of him he needs me.

What do they want to do with me Mommy he said. They want to have a doctor ask you some questions maybe give you a test just find out what you think about you're not crazy they just don't know you because you don't talk much in school they don't know you go to the library a lot they're annoyed that you read in class even though you get good grades. The doctor will find that all out and tell you it's okay and tell the principal all sorts of good things about you and they'll be nicer to you after that maybe you'll like school better too.

But the principal will have it in for me now especially after what you said they'll want to send me to another school.

Grownups don't hold grudges they can't afford to I said and they won't send you to another school but I hope you learned something you shouldn't have held it in for so long you should have told us so you wouldn't have to fight all that fighting does is just lead to more trouble that's where real trouble is because when you fight you get hurt and so you haven't solved the problem Willie's the sick one he needs special treatment.

Johnny and me were still talking we've never talked like this before when Dick came home rushed upstairs I heard drawers opening banging shut I told Johnny to go out and play Dick was packing rushing around pulling clothes out of drawers he couldn't even see what a mess he was making what are you doing? Getting the hell out of here don't play innocent you little slut independence my ass I found out what you do after work why didn't you do it before when you were home why wait till you're out working?

Don't you want to hear about your son my son?

What about him he's coming with me you're unfit to be his mother.

You're unfit to be his father he almost broke a boy's nose almost knocked his eye loose at school

He should've   should've killed him too if he had to.

You want your son to be a murderer listen you think you're Mr. Rung 2 or Rung 3 how many virgins have you had lately what have you been doing after those cocktail parties the late nights the other excuses you think I'm not wise?

What do you know you don't know you know how to spread your legs I never would've thought

And you're the model husband Mr. Faithful who's never cheated.

That doesn't matter.

Oh it doesn't so you're admitting you cheat on me always have and that's okay. I wish I could've said he was lying about you but he tricked me and I was foolish and weak but at least he wasn't lying I wish it would've been a lie so it would be all my fault but it wasn't I sobbed but then I cleared my head. You can brag to the boys about your running around it doesn't get back home because you're the perfect husband that's how men of this new higher social class prove themselves they're tired of just dickering over desks and file cabinets not doing an honest day's work anymore that's why the whole country's fucked up.

Don't use that language in my house he said.

They want psychiatry you go join the principal the whole country all our neighbors you take them all Johnny and me are leaving you take the house your two cars at least today I learned one thing no two things I learned I have a son who needs me I learned instead of a husband there's this stupid dick.

You're not only a slut you talk like a slut.

Sure it's big-man talk call me a slut a frail little delicacy like me my poor teeth will shatter if I utter a cuss word he just stood there watching me pack now I know what things I need where they are how to pack and then he grabbed my arm I pulled away my arm burned where he held me why don't you punch me a one-two combination you could knock me right through the drywall out onto the street why don't you prove how strong you are?

He dropped down on the bed wait a minute wait a minute something's wrong here really wrong I mean we've never talked this way before.

Wait for what all of a sudden you think you love me again even though I've been defiled?

I did love you you don't love me you wouldn't be cheating on me.

Cheating on me do you know how many times how many different men am I having an affair am I just putting out to have a good time? I started packing again I couldn't take it anymore I had to get away from this you're so sure you know what happened that it was almost the same as rape that it was painful.

Who's the bastard where I'll kill him I'll kill him

You don't even know you don't know even know if any of it's true but what about your women am I supposed to kill them to even the score?

He says look life's not that easy you know there are a lot of different forces at work constantly pushing you this way and that and sometimes it's hard or impossible to resist.

That was the first sensible thing I heard him say and I sat down too and waited for him to say more.

I'm not the strongest person in the world you don't know I couldn't begin to tell you what the rat race is like out there they're waiting for you to slip all the time with sharp knives they're lying to you constantly trying to see what you'll fall for trying constantly to take what you've got you're the fastest gun until a faster one comes along. Now you know all this and you forgive me you still love me don't you?

I don't know I don't know I need time to think I said. I'm numb from this and he didn't deny his cheating and I don't feel the pain yet and then I said yes I do love you because I really do I know he's a good man and tries hard.

You're the only woman I've ever loved I really mean it I'm sorry all those other things aren't important he put his arm around me kissed my neck I moved away Johnny will be back any minute he really needs us now you don't know what he's been through. I looked him in the eye this is the first time since when that we've talked look he needs us right now you need to talk to him to boost him up too not just you know go out there and beat up the world.

He's got to grow up to be a man not a

Yes I know but you know what I mean look this day you don't know what his school his principal you don't know what

I know I'm just too used to it I guess I take it all for granted well that's life ha-ha got to grin and bear it.

We heard Johnny come in downstairs I went down to make dinner and I felt the whole thing would settle I wanted it to settle so did Dick I had never had so many different emotions all at once but it was settled we weren't breaking up there was no reason even to separate for a while I felt this was home I was in the right place.

After dinner we went out to the Dairy Boat for sundaes and talked about different things and Dick asked Johnny if he wanted to try out for Little League this year it wasn't too late not at all that he'd help him practice pitch to him a lot so he could get a good swing it was better to play than to watch it on TV read books about it practice and hard work more than anything even the best players would tell you there was only so much ability and the rest was practice and Johnny looked at his father and said did you play in Little League and Dick said they didn't have it where I grew up but I played a lot with friends you know pickup games in the schoolyard somebody's dad would umpire until it was time for supper.

Those were the good old days Johnny said.

When Dick said what did you say we both looked at the kid and laughed.

Those were the good old days your mom didn't have to work your dad was always home for supper same time every night.

When he had work Dick said. Sometimes he didn't have work just hung around and neighbors thought he was a bum because he got laid off and built us a backboard in the maple tree and took us for rides in this old state patrol car he bought cheap and fixed up.

Then I went back on afternoon shift and stopped watching the stories just stopped altogether didn't try to find new ones either just quit but then tried the cartoons for a little relaxation on the portable while fixing dinner and never knew how funny in a silly way but funny they really were I mean I had a good time not great not every day but sometimes while fixing dinner. Johnny came in and said are you really watching the cartoons Mom I don't even watch them anymore and I said yes and he said are you crazy why and I said look the cat's after the mouse the wolf's after the bird the dog's after the rabbit they blow each other up fall off cliffs out of airplanes run through brick walls they're constantly beating up on each other killing each other really destroying everything and starting all over again. **Q**

Via delle Rose

When Rachel left her husband of many years, she would hardly have said her life was beginning. She had no family, few friends; she was drinking too much; she was falling apart.

Sometimes, unable to read, she would sit immobile at the window, listening to the sound of the bells tolling the hour and watching the swallows circle above her like dark specks of dust stirred up in the white sky. She would imagine the faces of people she had once known and, sometimes, even that of some mysterious stranger, in the shapes of the passing clouds. Finally, she would move, only to fill her glass and sink down on the bed, lying there heavily, restless, unable to sleep.

When the maid came in the morning, she would find the bedroom door still closed. She moved quietly around the apartment, pushing a soft damp cloth on the end of a brush across the cold tiled floor.

The maid, who was one of six children, probably liked the thick walls of the villa where Rachel had rented a floor, on Via delle Rose, though there were no roses on that street. Perhaps what the maid liked was the shuttered quiet of the first floor—what was known as the *piano nobile*—and the sheltered, sunny veranda with its creepers and potted plants, which she watered diligently all through the Roman winter, humming love songs softly to herself as she worked, so as not to disturb Rachel.

Eventually, sometime before noon, Rachel would call out, "I'm awake, you can bring in breakfast," or she would say, "Gray day, isn't it, Rosetta?" her pale face glimmering for a moment at the door.

Rosetta, who was a slight girl with knock-knees and a fresh, country face, would walk quickly into the kitchen and tie her apron strings twice around her small waist.

The maid served Rachel her breakfast of bread and coffee and fresh strawberries, when she could find them, on a tray in her bed. Rosetta would fold back the shutters, letting the sunlight into the room, and stand by the bed, while inquiring with apparent interest after Rachel's health. There was something about Rachel's daily description of her constitution, of her sleepless nights, a certain exotic quality, reinforced by the accented Italian, that probably fascinated Rosetta.

"I couldn't sleep for hours," Rachel might say, and wave a ringed hand, impatiently, in the air.

Rosetta would turn to Rachel and cluck her tongue with sympathy, though she could, no doubt, hardly imagine lying awake in a bed; when, her endless chores accomplished, she managed to get into hers, she always fell asleep immediately.

"My head aches terribly. My liver is shot already, and the doctors tell me it'll be the end of me if I go on drinking. But sometimes, when I wake in the morning and find all of myself still there—the arms, the legs, the head—you know, Rosetta, I have the feeling I'd really rather never wake again," Rachel would say, and laugh in her brittle way, and bring the conversation to an end there, by wiping the froth of the whipped milk from the fine, dark hair of her upper lip, delicately, with her lace handkerchief.

Occasionally, she would continue.

"Tout casse, tout lasse, tout passe," she might say, or something of that sort, and vague images of her past would come to her: the sun on a stone wall, a white azalea on a mantelpiece, a blue silk dressing gown hanging behind the bathroom door.

But she felt little, only the headache and the fear of not being able to sleep.

"My father almost died of a heart attack last winter," Rosetta might say, and shake all her thin fingers from her narrow wrist like leaves on a branch in the wind.

Rachel would chew on a piece of toast in the side of her mouth, as though the business of eating was distasteful to her. Or she picked at the luscious strawberries with her small, plump fingers, holding up the dead-ripe fruit to the light. Sometimes Rachel spoke with increasing bitterness, her voice rising. She spoke of her husband—his continuous infidelity; of men in general—their conceit, their cowardice; of the human race—its abuse of any position of power. Occasionally she ended by upbraiding Rosetta herself for some minor misdemeanor, shouting at her. She even accused the maid of stealing a silk blouse, which Rachel had probably forgotten she had given the girl. Once, at the height of her helpless furor, Rachel brought her fist down on the rose pattern of the plate, shattering the pottery, which flew across the floor in small pieces.

During all of this, Rachel was aware of the hopelessness of trying to explain to Rosetta whatever it was she was actually trying to explain. Often, with tears in her eyes, she concluded by simply grasping the maid's hand and squeezing her fingers and then sending the maid from the room precipitately. Afterward, Rachel would apologize for her outburst and ask Rosetta not to mention it to anyone.

"*A nessuno, non lo direi a nessuno,*" Rosetta would say. Naturally the maid told all the people in the palazzo that the American signora was mad, really quite out of her mind. The people in the palazzo began to treat Rachel with studied politeness when they met her on the steps. As for Rachel herself, she continued to sit at the window and watch the winter sky, waiting for spring.

The boy appeared as if by magic, like a frangipani bloom on a gray, leafless branch. Rachel had known his mother at school, a long time before. When the mother telephoned to say the boy was looking for a place to stay, Rachel imagined a small boy in short velvet pants—a red-cheeked, curly-headed child with a wide mouth and wide-spaced blue eyes.

But he was not a child at all, though he was not yet full grown. He stood with one foot behind the other, angular, almost bony, his chin lifted. He wore a gold earring dangling rakishly from one ear and his fair hair cropped close to his head, so that the bones of his face seemed almost angry, and his hair stood up, bristling about him.

He had, Rachel thought, the fresh, flushed cheeks of a young girl.

Perhaps it was because of the pale spring light on the veranda, or the odor of damp earth that rose from the dripping, tangled back gardens below, but the boy seemed quite beautiful to Rachel, particularly his eyes, which were large, dark blue, acquisitive, but at the same time sad.

"Why did you come to Rome?" Rachel asked.

"For the experience," the boy said almost challengingly.

She ought to have changed out of her white shirt, Rachel thought, rubbing at a spot on the collar.

"Friend of mine came here last summer. I won't tell you what happened to him," the boy added.

"What did happen to him?" Rachel asked.

"Actually, I only know what they say happened," the boy said. The boy lowered his gaze, gave Rachel a quick glance, and then lowered his eyes again. He was not as beautiful as his mother had been, but something incongruously girlish about the boy's face made Rachel smile.

As Rachel turned to show the boy the way down the steps and into the passageway, the boy's arm brushed accidentally against hers, and she drew back abruptly.

Rachel asked the boy how his mother was.

"Actually, she was against Rome. She wanted me to go to the beach," he said.

Rachel felt the tears come into her eyes. "I'll show you the room," Rachel said, and opened the door.

The room had no view, but looked over the quiet dark well of a courtyard. It was small but comfortably furnished, though, just then, somewhat in disorder.

The boy hesitated, standing on the threshold, checked, perhaps, by the fact that the bedcovers had been thrown back, exposing piles of freshly laundered, intimate apparel. It was a room that Rosetta sometimes used in the afternoons for the ironing.

"I told the maid to tidy this room," Rachel said, and swept up a pile of laundry with an angry gesture. I'll have to do something about Rosetta, Rachel thought. The girl seemed to feel it was sufficient to push the duster across the floor and make the breakfast.

The boy stepped into the room and sat down on the bed, looking around. "I like it as it is," he said, bouncing up and down on the mattress.

Rachel glanced at him uneasily.

When the boy had left to fetch his things, Rachel tied a scarf around her head and dusted the room thoroughly. She smoothed the sheets across the bed, letting her hands linger a moment on the pillow slip.

"He's seventeen," Rachel said the next morning.

"Big," Rosetta said. She made a fist and shook it in the air as she added, "Well developed for his age, is it not true?"

Rachel was thinking of his mother's smooth brown legs.

Rosetta shifted from one small foot to the other, and sighed. She asked Rachel if she would be responsible for the boy's laundry, his room. Would she have to make his bed? Would the boy eat in the house? "He's going to need some taking care of," Rosetta concluded glumly.

"That's true," Rachel replied slowly, as though the thought had just occurred to her, and finished her cup of coffee.

Rachel walked slowly across the sunlit room to the window.

The sky was a clear blue, the outline of the red roofs distinct. She filled her lungs with air easily and stood there, her hands on the windowsill, feeling almost dizzy, her dusky skin lit up.

Rachel had not been a beautiful adolescent. Her skin was too sallow, her cheeks too round—she couldn't resist sweet things—and her hands always slightly clammy. Her dark eyes seemed sullen, though lit up from time to time unexpectedly. Her thick, wavy, chestnut hair, which she caught back in a loose knot perched precariously at the nape of her neck, was her best feature. She wore clothes that were too tight for her, dressing untidily in shirts that had a way of riding up out of the waist of her clinging linen skirts.

She wanted to be a journalist, but was very soon impatient with the tedium of the profession. She married an Italian she met on an assignment instead, believing she had fallen passionately in love with him, losing ten pounds and abandoning her work.

The man, an impoverished aristocrat from Urbino, was probably fascinated by a certain sensuality in Rachel's movements, the smoldering quality of her gaze, the way she draped herself across a deck chair with heavy lassitude, and by her fortune, which was considerable, acquired by her father in the diamond business. Besides, she courted the count with insistence and married him despite or, perhaps, partly because of her family's strong disapproval.

This was how Rachel's father expressed his opinion of his new son-in-law: "Count no account," he said, and gave his daughter a liberal allowance but told her he no longer wanted her in his house. When he died, he left Rachel his fortune and a spectacular diamond collection, some of which—the diamonds that is—she kept in the top drawer of her dresser.

Rachel's mother said, "An Italian, a Catholic. He'll give all your money to the Pope; he'll make you bring your children up as Catholics," and muttered something darkly about nuns burying babies in the backs of convent gardens.

Anyway, Rachel remained childless, took good care of her money, and spent her time watching over her man, jealously, waiting for the first signs of infidelity.

Once, when her husband came back late at night, he found Rachel roaming the streets without a coat, looking for him. He caught sight of her and stood watching her for a moment in the shadows as she came toward him, hugging the walls, coming on with something wild and purposeful in her gait. It had begun to rain, a fine mist of rain, falling like dust under the lamplight. Rachel, when she saw the count, stopped still, with her thick hair falling loose around her face in restless curls, the rain on her face, her big, dark eyes lit up with anger, her shiny dress clinging to her heavy breasts.

"You know what you remind me of?" he said.

She raised her dark eyebrows in inquiry.

"Salome," he said, and laughed.

The boy did not seem particularly shy. He came and went to his classes with his books under his arm, concentrating, apparently, on his studies.

Two nights after he had moved in, Rachel watched him in the hall preparing to go out. He stood before the mirror, brushed his cropped hair back with the tips of his fingers, and then swung his leather jacket over his shoulder.

Rachel asked him if he would like to eat with her. "It must be expensive eating out all the time," she said.

He turned his head sharply and replied, "No thanks," so firmly it startled her. "If I eat with you once, I'll end up doing it every night," he said.

Rachel and Rosetta walked down the stone steps of the palazzo together.

Before the maid turned down a side street, Rachel caught her looking up at the darkening sky and then casting a quick, furtive glance back at her mistress, who went on walking down Via delle Rose, the wind blowing her hair into her eyes.

The girl was really afraid of her, Rachel thought. Rosetta had probably told the whole building her mistress was a drunk, although these days Rachel had been drinking less. Since the boy had been in the house, Rachel often left the apartment in the afternoons, walking slowly into the center of Rome, strolling through the sunlit streets, stopping to look up at the arch and curve of a Baroque church or letting her hand run under the cool water of a fountain on the corner of a street. Sometimes she climbed up to the Campidoglio to watch the sun set over the city, or lingered for a moment on the Spanish steps, gazing down at the boat-shaped fountain below. Occasionally, she even went as far as St. Peter's. She wandered around the vast church, her eyes lifted, taking in the smell of incense, the color of the cardinal's robes, the way the light came slantingly through the alabaster window. Once, she found herself covering her hair and genuflecting before an altar, crossing herself as the other women did, and then kneeling down in the shadows in silence—not praying, her eyes on the sweep of the gold baldachin, a bowed, dark head, the curve of a white marble bust.

Occasionally, on certain warm evenings, she did not go home for dinner but sat under the creeper of some outdoor trattoria, eating a plate of *spaghetti in bianco* and watching the swallows circle in the transparent blue sky.

She found herself avoiding the boy. She could hear him in the mornings banging away in the kitchen, getting his breakfast—probably spilling the milk, she thought—or coming in late at night well past midnight and playing his transistor radio loudly in his room.

He asked her questions too, rather rudely, she felt, questions like: "What do you *do* all day?" "Don't you ever get bored?" "Have you *never* worked?" "Do you always drink *whiskey* every night?"

And she didn't drink whiskey every night, she thought now, as she felt the first heavy drops of rain on her face. She turned then and retraced her steps. She would get her umbrella, she thought, going back up the stone steps slowly. She would go for a long walk in the rain. She had never minded the rain; in fact, she rather liked the sudden summer storms, the excitement of it all.

The rain began to fall heavily as she opened the door to the apartment. She could hear the rain coming down hard while she stood looking around for her umbrella. She noticed that her bedroom door was ajar. She was certain she had closed the door. She was almost certain she had locked it.

She walked quietly across the tiled floor of the living room, breathing heavily. She felt hot, and she was perspiring, her hands damp, as she pushed open the door.

In the gray, flickering light of the storm, the boy stood before the open drawer of her dresser, bending over slightly, with his back to her. She could see the back of his round, cropped head, like a fist.

"*What* are you doing?" she said.

When the boy turned and saw Rachel's face, he took two steps back, ducking his head to one side, as if to avoid a blow.

"How dare you!" Rachel yelled, her rage coming to her slowly as if from afar. As Rachel advanced on the boy, one arm raised to strike him, she could feel her head throbbing like the rain pounding on the window. The light seemed ashy around the boy, his smile coming and going across his face, his blue eyes dark, a deep violet. Suddenly he turned and bolted, so quick on his feet he startled Rachel, and she drew back.

The two women sat in the kitchen under the glare of the yellow light, listening to the sound of the rain and the ticking of the kitchen clock, waiting for the boy.

It was late, and he had been gone a long time.

"Perhaps I should go down into the street to see if I can find him. Where do you suppose he goes at night? Do you imagine he has a girl, or do you think he goes with the prostitutes?" Rachel asked.

Rosetta went on cleaning the silver cup with her big pink hands. She rubbed at the silver with slow, mechanical gestures, without looking up, shrugging her shoulders and pulling down the edges of her mouth and saying only *"Beh"* when Rachel looked at her inquiringly.

The girl was really no help, Rachel thought. She seemed to get slower and slower. From time to time, Rachel had found her just standing in the middle of a room, her wide mouth slightly open, a duster in her hand. Perhaps the girl was really a little touched in the head.

"Didn't you just clean that silver, Rosetta?" Rachel asked.

"It passes the time, signora," the girl said.

Rachel lifted her gaze to the ceiling.

There was a long pause.

Rachel said suddenly, pouring herself another drink, "Perhaps I should call his mother."

"What would you say to the signora?" Rosetta replied, looking up for a moment from the silver cup, blinking her clear gray eyes.

Rachel gave the maid a glance of surprise, because, after all, what on earth *would* she say to the woman? Even more to the point, she was afraid of what the woman might say to her, Rachel. The mother would be sure to ask what the boy was doing in the dresser drawer, and what *was* the boy doing in the dresser drawer? Perhaps he was simply looking for something—a pencil or a stamp. Or perhaps he simply wanted to see her things. Perhaps he was just curious.

"Would you like me to make some camomile tea?" Rosetta asked, sniffed, and went on polishing. She was on the spoons now, taking each one and holding it up to the light to make sure it was thoroughly clean.

Rachel shook her head, and poured another whiskey, and indicated the tissues on the shelf. The girl blew her nose loudly.

Rachel looked at her face, and thought suddenly that her

skin looked almost transparent, and that the girl was getting thinner. Her face was pinched. Her nose looked bony and a little red. Her big red mouth and her blank gray eyes seemed to take up all of her small face. Her striped uniform, though clean, hung on her shoulders. She was not an ugly girl, Rachel thought, but she'd probably never find a husband, poor thing. She wasn't quite sure what it was the girl lacked, something like vitality. There was vagueness about the girl, a certain passivity, a sort of resignation that irritated Rachel. When Rosetta had first come from the country to work for her, Rachel had found her fresh-looking and neat. She had grown quite fond of her. But she seemed to have lost her color in the town, grown absentminded in her work. Perhaps I have spoiled her, Rachel thought.

Rachel had a sudden desire to get up and take the girl by her shoulders and give her a good shake. Instead, she sighed and said, "Not that I really know very much about the boy. He's been in this house for over a month, and I know next to nothing about him. He doesn't say much. Keeps to himself most of the time, doesn't he? Who knows, perhaps he takes something, or he's got mixed up with some gang of thugs. Perhaps he's got some girl into trouble."

Rosetta put the spoon down and said in a voice as monotonous as the sound of the rain, "Cousin of mine fell into the hands of the Mafia. Never heard from him again."

"Good heavens," Rachel said, and shuddered. She added, "Of course anything's possible these days. But he always looks so innocent to me, isn't it true? It's those blue eyes. He has beautiful eyes, don't you think? He looks, not naïve, but innocent. And he has the soft skin of a girl. Have you ever noticed his skin?"

The maid shrugged her shoulders and pulled her mouth down at the corners and said, *"Beh?"* again, lifting her hands palms up to the ceiling.

Rachel said, "If you say *'beh'* once more, I'll scream."

Rosetta didn't say anything, but kept on polishing, her eyes lowered.

There was a long silence. Then Rachel said, "How could I have suspected?" letting her head sink down into her arms.

She felt ill. Her head ached terribly. She had a pain down her side, which might be the liver, she thought. She shouldn't have drunk so much whiskey. She thought of the Italian doctor, an elderly man with silver hair, saying to her, "You cut out alcohol absolutely or . . ." and snapping his long white fingers with an eloquent gesture in the air, looking grave. She had known exactly what he meant. She could even imagine it, her life going from her as easily as the snap of the doctor's white fingers.

Rachel lifted her head slightly and propped it on one hand and whispered, "Perhaps something terrible has happened to the boy, perhaps he's been hurt, perhaps he's lying somewhere, wounded, dead." She sat up completely and said dramatically, looking at Rosetta directly, clenching both fists, "Do you know, Rosetta, if I could have, I think I might almost have killed him at that moment."

"My father once almost killed one of my brothers, beat him to within an inch of his life," Rosetta said in her deadpan voice, as though killing people were the most ordinary thing in the world, and went on polishing the knives.

"Oh, for God's sake, Rosetta, stop polishing that silver, will you. I can't stand it any longer," Rachel said, and stood up and began pacing around the kitchen. She realized she was shouting. "Why don't you just go on home. Go on. Go home. There's really no point in your sitting there like a . . ." She tried to think of how to say "sack of potatoes" in Italian idiom and gave up. The worst was not being able to swear at the girl in English, she thought.

When the maid had gone, Rachel sat at the kitchen table and poured herself another drink.

. . . .

A cat was crying on the landing, the howl rising and falling in the night. Rachel lay her head down on the table again. Useless, she thought. She would never sleep until she knew what had happened to the boy, not even if she drank an entire bottle of whiskey. There was a noise then, the rattle of a sudden gust of wind on the windowpane, or perhaps the action of a key in the lock. The rain had stopped. She turned toward the door.

The boy walked into the room. He was wet, and breathing hard; he had probably been running; his eyes looked bloodshot. He stood at the other end of the kitchen table with his head hanging, his thin shoulders stooped, not looking at her but rubbing the tip of his finger on the table, catching his breath.

Rachel pushed back her loose hair from her face, adjusting her white gown over her breasts.

"I saw the light on in the kitchen, and I thought—" the boy said.

Rachel pulled the belt of her gown tighter around her waist and wet her lips.

The boy rubbed the oilcloth on the table, making it shine, but he wasn't looking at the table. Rachel watched his self-conscious movements.

"Do you want to sit down?" she asked.

The boy went on rubbing at a spot on the oilcloth. Then he crossed his arms across his chest, hugging himself, his head bowed. He'd got skinny in her house, Rachel thought.

"I suppose you're going to explain to me what you were doing?" Rachel said.

The silence between them was almost tangible. Rachel realized all her anger had gone now. She hunted for it, but she couldn't find it. Then, suddenly, she went to him and pressed his wet head to her shoulder. She stroked his head, feeling the stubby hair, the bones.

"It's all right," she whispered, hurriedly, senselessly.

He pulled away, looking down at her. "You don't understand, please. Don't talk," he hissed, his face close, his lips swollen, trembling. He said, "When I saw the light on, I thought you might be worried. I didn't want to . . ." He drew back from her.

She remembered she had not brushed her hair or put any makeup on her face. He must smell the whiskey on her breath. All her wrinkles must be visible under the harsh kitchen light. She turned away and smoothed back her hair. She reached out to him again and pressed him close to her, pushing his head against her shoulder, feeling his warmth begin to spread through her body.

He hung there limply, his eyes shut, apparently exhausted.

"I love you," she said to the boy, with tears in her eyes, her hot, whiskey breath on his neck.

"I shouldn't have come back. I was crazy," the boy said, but without moving, his body still resting against hers.

"I know how you must feel. I just wanted you to know."

"You don't know anything," the boy said, and pulled away from her.

She had a pain down her side. She looked at the boy, who slumped now into the kitchen chair where Rosetta had sat, his head in his hands, the water dripping from the end of his nose.

She told him to go and take off his wet things. She asked him if he was hungry, if she could make him some food. She felt suddenly ravenous. She had eaten nothing since the day before at lunch, she realized. The boy shrugged his shoulders, but rose and went to his room. She could hear the sound of the shower as she began to cook: eggs, bacon, a huge pile of toast. She squeezed oranges and grapefruits. She brewed coffee and heated the milk. When she called the boy for breakfast, he was in his blue pajamas, his cheeks red, his hair sticking up around his head like a blond halo, Rachel thought.

Rachel had laid the kitchen table with a clean white cloth

and spread the breakfast out. The boy sat down and began to eat. He ate slowly at first, and then with increasing speed, one slice of toast after the other, three fried eggs—dipping the bread into the eggs, slices and slices of bacon with his fingers. Rachel sat and ate beside the boy, buttering the slices of toast in silence.

Through the kitchen window, the sky grew light over the ancient city. The terra-cotta façades, the pink-and-white azaleas, the stray cats, the fountains, the stones of the churches emerged once again out of the night.

After that, the summer months slipped by easily, like smooth beads through the fingers of her hand, despite the heat, which gradually increased as they approached August. Afterward, Rachel thought that she could probably have gone on like that forever, almost happy.

She rose early, bathed, and dressed carefully in fresh cotton dresses with gaily colored, high-heeled sandals and handbags to match. She went to market before the heat of the day. She bought bright fruits: strawberries, peaches, plums; vegetables and flowers; fish and meat. She touched the fruit and vegetables carefully, as she had seen the neighborhood Italian women do. She observed the eye of the fish to be certain of its freshness. She had the vendor cut into the watermelon and tasted a slice on the street, bending over so as not to spill the juice down the front of her dress. She came home laden down, her straw baskets filled. She cooked breakfast for the boy, even bringing him his eggs and bacon in bed on the weekends, with freshly squeezed juice and a flower on the tray.

The boy ate all his meals at home, eating copiously. He had an appetite that made Rachel laugh. She wondered how he had managed to feed himself all through the first month he had spent in her place.

In the long, hot afternoons they sat together on the veranda with the orange awning drawn down, casting a pinkish shade. The boy sat with his feet crossed on the railing of the veranda, his hands behind his head. Rachel helped him with his Italian. He left the book unopened on his knees and asked her for certain useful phrases.

At first he asked her for the exact names of the parts of the body, how to order a dinner, how to buy things in a shop. Eventually he asked her directly for words of love. Laughingly, she taught him what she had learned from the count. Gradually they began to talk in Italian, the boy haltingly and Rachel increasingly spontaneously. She told him about her childhood, her friendship with his mother, her life with the count.

"Now, he was a good lover. Anything went," she said, and opened up her arms in a gesture of acceptance.

The boy lifted his eyebrows appreciatively and smiled with complicity.

Rachel wondered what he knew about the art of love.

In the autumn, when the boy had gone, Rachel took to walking the streets alone, unable to sleep in the early mornings, amazed at the industry at that early hour. In the shadows of the dawn, the streets wet and glistening, bakers baked bread and butchers cut up meat. She stopped once and watched, fascinated, while a butcher with a bloodstained apron carried an entire carcass of some animal over his shoulder. At times she realized she was talking to herself, her lips moving silently.

One morning, when she came back from market to Via delle Rose early, she went into the kitchen and found Rosetta already there. The girl was sitting by the window in the sun, gazing out at the bright sky, her dark hair tied back from her face, her big mouth slightly open. She had thrown her head back with her chin lifted, and the clear sunlight was on her face and her chest. Her skin looked transparent. Rachel followed the line of her neck to her full breasts and down to her thickened waist.

The girl, seeing Rachel staring, started and got up. She walked across the kitchen to Rachel slowly, awkwardly.

Rachel went on staring, her eyes on what she must have seen but not recognized before.

For a moment, the two women stood in silence, facing one another, the girl looking down at the pool of sunlight on the stone floor and Rachel looking down at her.

"Poor girl, poor dreamer," Rachel said, for the girl and for herself, and patted the maid on the shoulder. **Q**

After the Stations of the Cross

[1]

I was the definition of toast in the aisle with all the cereals and I had my fixing goggles on the sweet ones when I heard some dude go, Robbie. This is my name, so I of course checked it out, but all that was there was this one dude stamping price tags on boxes of Cheerios, so I was ready just to bag it and think it was just my brutal toastedness and my ears fucking with me, when I saw that the dude stamping price tags on boxes of Cheerios was looking like I was supposed to say something back to him, so I figured it was him who said it, even though I didn't have a shit's clue as to who this dude was. It fucking took forever to figure it out, too, and this all because of his feathery blow-dry neat-look hair job, and the apron and tie and fashion-tight pants, and the pointy-toed pimp shoes that made him look like some whole different type of dude altogether. So here I was, about to try to say something back to some dude who looks like he knows me when I know I don't know him, when I notice he's got this tattoo hanging out on his arm, where he's got his sleeve rolled up, of some dude hanging casual on one of those one-seater mini-cartoon floating desert islands with the one palm tree, and he's sipping with a straw from a cut-in-half coconut. This tattoo I hadn't seen since shop class senior year, on a dude named Chuckie Goldman, and I can tell you right now it's the only thing that's stayed the same.

See, back then he was a textbook burnout, with the biker boots and the bell-bottoms and the big-mother black leather wallet the size of a payroll check that he chained to his belt with the bottle-opener buckle. Really, the only difference between Chuckie Goldman and every other burnout dude was where when every other burnout had his black concert T-shirt with *Black Sabbath* or *Judas Priest* on it, Chuckie Goldman and his buddies had something different, because of this gang they had they called The Sons of Satan, so that they custom-printed *The Sons of Satan* on the backs of their black T-shirts, and so that they got this iron-on of a black leather biker dude and a nude foxy mama on a floating Harley surrounded by clouds and by big Bible letters that said, SWORN TO FUN, LOYAL TO NONE on the front. Chuckie Goldman and his buddies all had that scummy heavy-metal burnout hair and the chocolate-milk mustaches, and on the backs of the black leather jackets they wore, it said *The Sons of Satan,* too. Chuckie Goldman also had this big black van with bubble windows in back, and he cruised all The Sons of Satan around in it, and so I just always figured he was Big Cheese with The Sons of Satan, even though I really never had a shit's clue what The Sons of Satan ever did besides hanging behind the boiler room by the Bio pond before school and at lunch, blowing the doobage with all the other burnouts. Really, if you want to know the truth, all I ever really knew about Chuckie Goldman was that he made a metal bong in my shop class senior year, and that he sold my buddy Spooge smokables like he still does now, and that he had the same tattoo then as he did when I saw him stamping price tags while I was such toast in the grocery store.

So when I knew who he was, I went, Hey, dude, what's the hap?

He went, Having a bash at my place tonight.

This bash at his place, I figured, would be to the fucking gills with the type of dude like Chuckie Goldman is, who were burnouts then but now are all decked out and filling bags for somebody's mother, or collecting carts in the parking lots, or whatever the shit ex-burnouts working at grocery stores have to do—since, besides Spooge, the only other dudes I know of around here that didn't go away someplace to school are the type of dude like Chuckie Goldman is.

I went, Big bash?

He stamped another price tag on another box of Cheerios and went, Well, sort of, but it's bring-your-own. Need directions?

Since Spooge has been buying smokables from the dude, I went, Spooge knows how to get there.

Chuckie Goldman went, Cool.

Then he went right on back to stamping more price tags, so I figured he was as much of a toast bandit as I was and couldn't think of jackshit to say, so I went back to the sweet-cereal scene and copped myself some Lucky Charms and chucked them in the cart and went, Check you out later, dude. Then I cruised my cart to the checkout line when I really should have checked out the Beauty and Health Aids and Feminine Needs aisle to get some sunscreen and Chap Stick for the Claw, which was the big reason I was there in the first place, since the Claw was running late and still packing and didn't have time to get it herself before the airport limo came, and she was crawling up my ass, calling me lazy lummox and having a fucking cow and making me go shopping for her sunscreen and Chap Stick, and also for chow for me and the Embryo for when she and the Old Man booked on vacation. So the Claw gave me cash, and since the fake-wood wagon was in the shop, the Claw gave me the Old Man's BMW keys, which I took and booked, cruising along in luxury, cranking tunes and blowing some of the mind-stop that Spooge got from Chuckie Goldman, all of this explaining why I was such serious toast in the grocery store and forgot to get the sunscreen and Chap Stick after hearing about the bash, and was completely clueless about it until the Claw blew me the major pies when I got home.

[2]

The Claw went, Selfish, thoughtless, good-for-nothing! What *is* this! Sweet cereal and frozen *pizza*? You do this to *spite* me! You can't even do me this *one thing*! Let me see your eyes! *Let me see them!* So, how many puffs of marijuana smoke *today,* Robbie? How many puffs from that water pipe that I happen to know that you're hiding? Oh, your *father* will be *very* happy to hear about *this* when I meet him at the airport. How does it *feel* to know you've ruined our whole vacation, *hmmn*? I should just call it *all* off, just *call* it off! How would you feel about *that,* hmmn? *Oh,* of *course,* I for*got,* you're *far* too drugged on that marijuana smoke to feel *anything,* aren't you? Oh, to *think* I could be so *foolish* as to trust *you* to watch over your little sister! It's *she* who should be doing the watching!

Well, I guess that's about enough of the Claw's rag treatment action. Besides, she had to finish varnishing her hair dome, and then got distracted when the Embryo came squealing down the stairs, going, Mother! Mother! Look at me! Look! and spinning around like the Barbie doll she is in her peach-puke cotton-candy Homecoming dress, and it's of course the exact type of Easter egg afterbirth the Claw eats right up.

The Claw was going, Oooooo! *Don't* you look *nice*! That is *just* the *cutest* little *dress*!

You can bet there was too much cheese flying around for me to deal on, so I booked to the kitchen and copped myself some Lucky Charms and milk and cruised with it into the TV room, where I cooked through the channels, with it mostly just news on, until I found a rerun of *The Flying Nun,* which I hung with and got casual. During this part I was watching where the Flying Nun needed to take off and cook around but couldn't because of her flying powers being fucked somehow, I heard this car horn honking outside the TV room window. I looked out and saw this big-mama black stretch job of a limo hanging out there in the half-circle driveway, and whoever the fuck the lame-assed dude behind the smoked glass was was laying on the goddamn horn like he just drove up in a cab.

I yelled in to the Claw, going, You pay this dude to come honk his horn?

The Claw went, Shut your smart mouth, young man, and take my bags out there. Pronto!

Now, I could've tried to crawl up her ass, just to do it, but I figured she'd only blow me some more pies, so I swallowed my pride and went and got her three heavy-as-shit suitcases from the front hall and booked with them out to the big black stretch job honking in the driveway. Let me tell you, it was cold enough out there to make your scrotal sac shrivel up and goose-pimple, and whoever the lame-assed dude behind the smoked glass was seemed to know it, because he didn't even get out to give me a hand, he just popped the trunk open from inside. I gave the smoked glass a fuck-you look and chucked the Claw's shit in the trunk and shut it. I started cruising in when the Claw cruised out, looking something fierce in her foofy fur coat and giving me the silent business like she thought it would break my heart. Then she just got in and slammed the door behind her and was gone to the airport, where she and the Old Man would fly away to where I wouldn't have to see them for a week.

Don't think this upset me, it was extremely suitable, but still, when I stood there in the driveway with it almost completely dark out and my arms folded in that brutal nip-chilliness in just jeans and a T-shirt, I couldn't help getting boged-out, because I was feeling like I was stuck down in this stupid house in this little dinky island of a town with nothing but some mind-stop for this whole fucking week off I got from flipping meat at one of the Old Man's Sizzlers to babysit the Embryo. Then I started getting boged-out about the fact that winter and snow and shit were coming soon, ever since the leaves got orange and fell, and I got boged-out about it being so shiver-assed cold, which made me think what the fuck was I doing standing in the driveway in just jeans and a T-shirt and freezing when I'd be much better off inside, where it was at least warm, so I started heading back in, and I put my hands in my pockets, and I just about shit my pants, because in my one pocket I still had the keys to the BMW that the Claw forgot to ask for back.

[3]

All fired up about the keys like I was, I figured I'd go in and ring up Spooge and tell him about it, which I tried to do, but the Potato picked it up and told me she'd have him call back, because he was hanging on the throne, which was what I half expected, seeing as half his waking hours are spent trying to lay some cable and he's always at it whenever I call.

So I hung up and got casual again with *The Flying Nun* and picked up my Lucky Charms to finish them off, but they'd been hanging so long they'd turned to mush, and I had to bag the whole idea and torch up a square instead, which I was smoking while I watched the last part of *The Flying Nun* when the Embryo came in and stood right in front of my view of the TV, going, Where is my lipstick? Where did you put my lipstick?

I went, What the fuck do I look like here, Mr. Encyclopedia King? Get out of my face, I'm trying to watch the TV.

So the Embryo went, Fine, A-hole, how about I just tell Mother I caught you smoking in the house? How would you like that, you big fat jerk?

I went, Eat my shorts, tight-assed bitch. Then I expectorated with vigor, without letting it fly, just as a warning so she'd think I had a good juicy greenie coming and she'd get the fuck out of my way.

She went, Gross! You fat pig! But she moved out of my way and I thought it did the trick, until she went to the phone behind me and called up some tight-assed bitch friend of hers and started walking around the room with the phone in her hand in her peach-puke cotton-candy Homecoming dress, making these swishing noises and going off in her loud-assed stupid whiny fuck socialite voice, like all of a sudden she's turned into a Jewish chick.

Let me tell you, when the Embryo gets into this action, it's way beyond the valley of unacceptable, where she's going, Omi*god*! I mean, I'm like, omi*god*! I like, *totally* can't even *believe* that! I mean, Todd is like *way* cute. I mean, he's like, *so* totally cute, he's like, totally *way cute.* For *sure.* Wait, you *did*? Omi*god*! I *know*! Totally! Omi*god*! *Missy,* you're like, *so* totally *lucky*! I *swear,* I'm like, *totally* like, omi*god*!

I hope you get the idea of how brutal that can be, and how it's hard to keep yourself from projectile yacking, and how you have to shout, Shut the fuck up! which I did and she didn't, but instead made the nearly fatal mistake of trying to wedge her way even deeper up my ass by putting her puke-assed dress right in my line of watching the end part of *The Flying Nun,* on purpose, which I wasn't about to sit there and deal on, so this time none of this nice-guy fake hocker bluffing action, this time I let a really truly vicious hunk of brutal lung cheese come cooking up my throat and wing out end over end like those good heavy ones always do, and she was fucking lucky she got out of the way, too, because when it slapped against the TV and went gooping down the Flying Nun's face, it didn't look like something you'd want hanging out on your Homecoming dress, and that's for fucking sure.

And so of course the Embryo had to start going, *Eeeeew*! *Eeeeew*! *Gross*! You're *sick*! You gross *pig*! It's my fat A-hole brother, and he like, *spit* at me! You're lucky you missed, *A*—hole, you're just *lucky*! Missy, I'm like, wearing my dress? Yeah, and my A-hole brother *spit* at it! Isn't that the *grossest*? Get out of here, gross *pig*! I'm telling Mother on you!

I cashed my square in my Lucky Charms and went, Go ahead, you little ax wound. Then I booked into the kitchen and chucked the bowl into the sink, and I looked up and saw the picture hanging there above it of the Claw and the Old Man in their stupid-looking ski outfits, smiling at the camera, with their arms around each other and the mountains big behind them. I went, Fuck you, too.

[4]

Right then the doorbell went off in the front hall, and I could hear the Embryo on the phone in the TV room going, Omi*god*! He's *here*! I'm so totally *psyched*! Gotta *go*! Then I could hear her puke-assed dress swishing toward the front door, and I could hear her shout, Clean off the TV, fat pig! Then I heard her open the door, sounding just like the Claw when she answers the phone with her velvet voice. Then the phone in the kitchen started ringing and I picked it up and it was Spooge.

I went, Hey, dude, how'd it go?

Spooge went, How'd what go?

I went, Weren't you eating a rat?

This was a big hairy fat-assed boner on my part, because I was forgetting that Spooge takes his ka-kas very seriously, getting all into a fucking sweat about the shapes and sizes and textures of the things, and going off about them like they're his parents or something. Like he'll go, Today my stool was a kind of a dark yellow and kind of like soft serve and it had whole pieces of corn in it that I ate last night. Or he'll go, Today I had really bad Hershey squirts and the upshot is, it gave me ring of fire and now it hurts like hell to walk. And he'll go on and on, too, if you don't stop him and go, Spooge, listen, I know you like to stand up after laying some cable and look at it in fine-assed detail and let it tell you all about what kind of day you're going to have, but really, I really wouldn't be all that offended if you decided you wanted to keep that part of your life a secret from me. Like right then, when I'd pulled the boner and asked him how his rat-eating session went, Spooge went, Well, I've been feeling rather costive lately, so today after my psychology class, when I was downtown at school, I went into the cafeteria and bought a bran muffin, because it's said that bran muffins increase your regularity, and so when I got home here and took my shit, it was really very painful, and it looked just like this hard little bran muffin, only it was quite a bit darker.

I went, Spooge, that's nice. Thanks for sharing. Now listen. Then I told him about seeing this Chuckie Goldman dude earlier at the grocery store and how he told me he was having a bash and how the Claw booked without taking the keys to the BMW with her. So Spooge said to come on over to do some bongs, since we couldn't do them here because of the Claw crawling up my ass about the goddamn things ever since I got the boot from Culver Military Academy sophomore year for getting caught smoking one in my room. Spooge doesn't have to worry about getting caught smoking his, because his units are casual and their bedroom is downstairs and Spooge's is up and they never go up there, and even if they did and caught him tooting on the thing, they probably wouldn't care.

I asked Spooge if he had any drinkables and he said he didn't, so I hung it up and booked up the back stairway to my bedroom and got my half-full bottle of Jack from the rain gutter outside my window. I put it in my coat pocket and put on my coat and was about to book down the front stairway when I saw what was standing there down at the bottom in the front hall, looking at this framed-certificate thing the country club gave the Old Man when they made him the Big Cheese hanging on the wall. It was this dude who I figured must've been the Embryo's date for the dance, and he was looking at that framed-certificate thing like he thought it was hot shit. This dude was a serious dweeb, looking just like one of those dudes that was going to grow up to be one of those dudes that I used to caddy for when I used to caddy, the type of dude that wears super-bright green pants and a bright red sport shirt and shiny-like-new white shoes, the type of dude that tips you only a dollar fifty for eighteen holes and gets you a hot dog instead of a hamburger at the halfway house. He was holding this little white box, which I figured must've been the Embryo's flower, and he looked like such a weenis with his hair slicked back and his little bow tie that I almost felt sorry for him in the same way that I feel sorry for my little brother, thinking about him marching around in those brutal stiff black uniforms and twirling his rifle in the air and standing like at attention with a pole up his ass and dying to please. So you can see why I didn't want to talk with this dude. He looked to me like the kind of dude that would call you big guy, and to be called big guy would've been a bit too much for me to deal on.

So I went around and down the back stairway instead, booking out the back door by the covered swimming pool, cruising along the back of the house and through the back door of the garage, where the Old Man's BMW was waiting with its stupid-assed custom-job license plates that say EAT OUT in reference to the six Sizzler Steak Houses that the Old Man owns. It's hard to believe the Old Man could be so clueless and not know what people will take it to mean. They might as well just say 12 INCHES. The fake-wood wagon that was in the shop has custom-plate jobs, too, saying SKI BUM, which is what the units have flown off to be for the week. But even though the plates on the BMW are much more brutal, it's a much more suitable car, and I never get to drive the fucking thing, either. So I had a seat and sunk down in the furry white bucket dealies, shutting the door behind me and popping the engine, pressing the garage-door opener clipped to the sun shield and booking backward out the driveway, pressing it to Shut as I cruised down the street.

Like it always is with these expensive foreign jobs, it's so vacuum-packed quiet that you can't hear a thing, not even the engine, and there were no streetlights and it was black outside and I hadn't even popped the headlights yet, so it was like floating fast in a big black hole. When I popped them on, everything got grounded, and it looked pretty spooky out there, with these fucked-up shadows flying around the trees as I booked past, and these black shapes of houses floating by so smooth and quiet, and not jackshit in sight. I must've still been kind of toasted, because it was spooking me out in a weirdassed way, so I popped on the radio and cranked some tunes and concentrated on the orange glow of the dashboard lights until things seemed suitable again, and the next thing I knew, I was cruising up Spooge's driveway.

[5]

I threw it in park by the garage behind the house and got out and walked up to the back door. There was a window in the door, and I looked inside through it, and the whole downstairs looked dark, but then I saw this orange-tipped square burning off in the distance, so I knocked and the orange tip got up and came to the door and let me in, and I shut the door behind me. It was the Potato, and she went back to where she was, toward the table in the kitchen in the dark.

The Potato went, Hey, Robbie.

I went, Hey, what's the hap?

The Potato went, Nothing. Bored. Then she had a seat again at the kitchen table in the dark and kept on smoking her square and not saying anything. She's always there, smoking in the dark, when I come over, just like Spooge is always upstairs doing bongs and cranking tunes, and just like their units are always in the front room by the front door that nobody ever uses, watching the TV.

I went, Bored, huh?

The Potato just sort of laughed, like she was doing it in her sleep, which is exactly how she talked, too. Maybe it had something to do with what Spooge told me about some buddy of hers going down to Mexico and bringing back a shitload of prescription Valiums for her, but that might only be part of it, because she'd seemed like that ever since she'd dropped out of school a few months before that. Spooge told me that mostly she'd just hang out all day, stoned shitless and watching soaps and fingering peanut butter out of the jar in her sorority T-shirt and sweats, and then at night hanging at the kitchen table in the dark, smoking squares and smoking squares.

What's fucked up about all this is that she used to be pretty hot, and that there she was that night, looking like death and getting all fat, and all because of this one dude she did the boyfriend scene with for almost six years, this dude from around here named Bruno Pasquarelli, better known as Bruno I'm an Idiot Pasquarelli, of the Pasquarelli Construction family fame, the studly gold-chain guido pimp-shoes type of Italian dude that you'd figure his type of name would make him. She started doing the boyfriend scene with him back in high school, and then they went away to school together, and they ended up going out for almost six fucking years, until right when the Potato dropped out, which Spooge told me happened because of this Bruno dude selling blow.

Spooge told me this Bruno dude sold blow to most of the frats there, and that he used to hose a good number of the sorority chicks, too, but that the Potato didn't really give a shit, as long as he kept her blowhound tooter full. Thing was, she was such a blowhound that she started looking like one of those starving little African dudes that you always end up seeing if you come home late and toasted and you pop on the TV, and there they are, the kinds with the fucking flies hanging out on their lips. Apparently Bruno didn't get into that look, so he dropped her, and because he dropped her, she dropped out of school, and only two months from graduation, which is something even I wouldn't do if I'd gotten that far. I figured she must've had her reasons, though, because when I saw her when she came home after Bruno dropped her and she dropped out, she was pretty major fucking spooky action, like those brutal-looking dudes you see in those pictures of concentration camps.

[6]

It took her about a month to start looking normal again, and right about the time she did and started looking hot before she started getting fat, she and Spooge and me went out to this lame-assed bar they have around here called the Cattle Company, where all the ex-burnout grocery dudes hang out, and where all the swinging divorced chicks hang out, and where all the chicks wear their pants so tight that their crotches look like camel toes. I don't have a clue why we were there, because we'd been there once before and we knew it was beyond the valley of being unsuitable, but there we were, hanging, drinking beers in this one part that's supposed to look like a corral or some such shit, watching all these pathetic weenises doing the boogie-shoes scene like the hurting units they were on this dinky little lit-up-from-under dance floor while the lame-assed DJ played this tortured elf music with a disco beat. By the time we booked out of there, we were all pretty much toast bandits, but especially Spooge, because when we went back to Spooge's room for a bong session, Spooge took one down that would've made a house explode, and as he let the smoke fly and it hung above our heads, he fell back on his bed with the bong in his hand and was passed-out toast just like that. I had to cook over there and grab the bong from him, because he was about to spill the soup from it all over himself. If you've ever smelled bong soup, you'd thank me if you were Spooge, because the shit smells worse than the crust on your underwear.

So it was me and the Potato, laughing about Spooge sawing wood like a banshee, like the lightweight he was. When we finally stopped laughing, we just sat there and didn't say a thing, I guess because we couldn't think of anything to say. What was wigging me out, though, was that the Potato was hanging there on the floor next to me and smiling like I was Bruno I'm an Idiot Pasquarelli and not me. Obviously this wasn't the case, though, because then she started talking to me about him, and it was out of bounds, because out of the blue she started telling me about the first time she and Bruno hosed, when they were in their senior year of high school, in the other bedroom up there, on the Potato's pink-cotton-candy canopy bed, while Mrs. Spooge was downstairs cooking up dinner. She told me that neither of them had hosed before, and that neither of them had a shit's clue what to do, and that

Bruno had such a humongous husker that it hurt, and this whole time she was going off, I was hanging there with this shit-eating grin and not saying jackshit, because what the fuck do you say, and plus I was such toast I thought this was some kind of an invitation, even when she started saying that she never really even liked having sessions anyhow, even though she looked kind of bummed.

When she was finished talking about it, she just sat there like a wet puppy hanging out in the middle of a road, waiting for a truck to come and run it over. There wasn't anything I could think of to say, and besides, she all of a sudden moved over closer to me and put her head on my shoulder, right there on my fucking shoulder, and what else was there I was supposed to do? So I of course took her head in my hands and started playing kissy-face with it, and it was fine, too, it was suitable, and it went on for a pretty good long time, with the only sound being Spooge sawing wood, until I tried to go for the old titty action and knew I'd fumbled the ball in a big way.

She pulled away from me like she all of a sudden realized who the fuck I was, and that I sure as shit wasn't Bruno I'm an Idiot Pasquarelli, and she went, No.

I went, Are you sure?

She didn't say anything then, just sat there fixing her goggles on her hands in her lap like she was autistic, and I looked at her and listened to Spooge sawing wood, which sure as shit didn't help my chances any in the romantic-mood department.

Finally she went, I think you better go.

I went, Sure about that?

She just kept on staring at her hands and didn't say jackshit, and I, not being the type of dude that will beg just to get his end wet, booked.

[7]

When I got outside, though, I for some reason didn't feel much at all like hopping in the old fake-wood wagon with the SKI BUM plates and cruising home. I instead, for some reason, walked over to the fence that runs alongside Spooge's driveway and jumped it to where the Infant Jesus of Prague School playground is, the playground for where me and Spooge used to go to grade school, where I went until seventh grade, when my units made me go to Culver. When I landed on the ground on the other side, I cruised over to the swings and hung out there by them, looking up at the Potato's bedroom window until I saw the light go out there. Then I took out a square and torched it, and went around and had a seat on the middle swing facing Infant Jesus of Prague with my back to Spooge's house. Across the softball field from the playground, Infant Jesus of Prague sort of looked like it was a castle on an island, because of the fact that it stood alone on a hill, and that the street curved around it and surrounded it like a moat, and that the fence that went alongside Spooge's house separated it from everything else, and that on that night, it looked so huge in the darkness, even though it still didn't look so huge as when we were little dudes and were so wigged out by the Nazi nuns that we called it International Japanese Prison because of the initials being the same. It's a pretty ruthless building, an old brownish-red brick three-story job with black metal fire escapes and big-mother windows, and they shut it down just last year, I guess because of a shortage of Catholic kids or something. I heard last week that they're tearing it down to the ground soon, heard it when the Claw was reading *The Star* to the Old Man at breakfast before they booked for their golf game and before I went to toss meat around at the Old Man's Sizzler. The Old Man just about popped a hemorrhoid when he heard that, because he grew up around here and went to grade school there just like me, and he started going off about how he was going to protest it at the next Jaycees meeting, while he salted his eggs with his elephant salt shaker. I have to admit I was kind of wigged when I heard about it, too, but probably not for the same reasons as the Old Man. He probably misses the nuns winging erasers at him and trying to peg him with their long-assed rulers, where I'm just going to miss the building. It's a pretty suitable building.

Like that night when the Potato told me to book and I was hanging on the swings, that night Infant Jesus of Prague was looking like a castle in a very big way. That night I was hanging on the swings and smoking a square, the sky behind Infant Jesus of Prague was this kind of orange color, like this kind of a black-orange color, because of the lights from the city way off making it that way, and it pretty much drowned out the stars. Infant Jesus of Prague was like this jumbo black shadow against this blackish-orange sky, and the only detail of it you could see was that part of the fire escape sticking out on that one side, that same part of the fire escape that Sister Thomas Annette took a gravel dive off of when I was in third grade.

It was when Roy Spitzig, who was my best buddy at that time, was tossing Spooge's Twinkie as a joke around the gym where we ate lunch, and Spooge got all bent out of shape and went and told on him to Sister Thomas Annette, who was our lunch guard or something like that, hanging out all the time in her black robed nun getup, and she caught Roy by the collar and took Spooge's Twinkie from him and shoved the fucking thing in his face, and it had this white cream shit coming out of it by this time from it being tossed around, and she was shoving it in his face, going, Eat it! Eat it! And Roy wigged and slugged her in the gut and booked out of the lunchroom, and Sister Thomas Annette didn't seem to be hurt by that punch, because she booked right out of there after him.

Roy told me that Sister Thomas Annette finally cornered him in this one classroom on the third floor with that fucked-up Twinkie still in her hand, and she was still going, Eat it! Eat it! Roy told me that he was right next to the door to the fire escape, and so he opened it and went out there and started going down it. Sister Thomas Annette followed him out there, and if you don't believe that, believe it, because Sister Thomas Annette had flaming orange hair and a face like Ernest Borgnine with a potato chip wedged up his ass. Roy told me that when he got down to the bottom of the fire escape and had no place else to go but to jump, he turned around and looked up and saw Sister Thomas Annette coming down at him with that fucked-up Twinkie still in her hand, coming down that final flight, when the heel of one of her little black nun boots got sucked right down in between the rungs, and she screamed, Holy Jesus! loud enough that we could hear it from the lunchroom, where we were wondering what was going down up there, where it turned out it was Sister Thomas Annette, because it was then that she fell one flight down right on her flaming orange head.

Roy told me that the way it looked to him, it looked like Sister Thomas Annette was being pulled down to the ground really slow, or like she was a big black bomb he was watching fall through the sky from a plane high up, and that after that he would have these brutally bad dreams about falling nuns calling out his name. I'll tell you, I can't say I wouldn't either if I were him, because when Sister Thomas Annette took that gravel dive right down on her flaming orange head, she was turned right into a vegetable not too much different from what the Potato turned into when she dropped out of school and started smoking squares in the kitchen in the dark, there where I was hanging with her that night, listening to her laugh like she was laughing in her sleep.

[8]

I went, Spooge upstairs?

The Potato kind of nodded and made this grunting type of noise, like she was holding back a really good ta-fa, and just sat there looking at the square in her hands on the kitchen table, glowing in the dark, and I stood there, too, for a little while, with my goggles fixing on the orange tip of it there. Then I went, Yeah, well, check you out later, and booked out of there through the dark dining room, being not noisy so Spooge's units wouldn't hear me and I wouldn't have to get sucked into a flying-cheese session with them. I cracked open the door to the upstairs part, and it was all dark there, too, but I could hear the cranking of tunes from up there, so I took a grab at the railing and made my way up like a blind dude, stepping over all the piles of folded clothes and shit until I made it to the top, where down at the end of the hall I saw light from inside Spooge's room falling out into the darkness. I took my half-full bottle of Jack out of my coat pocket and walked down and into his room, sloshing it around in the air, but when I got in there, I saw Spooge hanging on the floor in his fucking undies with the big bong between his legs and the long round tube going up to his mouth, where he was working on woofing a lungful of mind-stop that was bubbling through the bong soup from the bowl he was torching. The dope glowed to ash as he slipped his thumb off the carb and the smoke slammed out of sight, Spooge taking away his mouth and squinting up his eyeballs and turning sort of purple as he popped the bowl off and cashed it in the ashtray.

I went, Bonging savage!

Spooge jerked up quick and coughed like he was yacking, and a mind-stop cloud came at me like those time-lapse clouds you see cooking across the sky in those encyclopedia science flicks that they showed us when we were in high school. When the smoke stopped coming, Spooge kept on coughing, and when he stopped that he went, Hey, dude.

He didn't say jackshit after that, he just was hanging there with a vicious case of bottle mouth, picking with his fingers at the red, white, and blue shag carpeting on his floor, so I had a seat on his bed and went, Toasting out, dude. Get a grip. Then I unscrewed the Jack and had a couple visits with it.

After a while, Spooge looked up and went, What? with this palsy-lipped smile, making this noise like somebody stirring macaroni and cheese.

I went, Check it out, sort of sloshing the half-full bottle of Jack around in the air in front of the toast bandit, just to check out if he was still alive, sort of like I used to hold up slices of pizza and other human food in front of my good old now-dead dog Taffy, with the scabs on the back, just to see if it was still kicking there in its plaid basket in the laundry room. I could tell Taffy still had it when it made some noises like its lungs were full of mud, just like I could tell Spooge still had it when he talked about his turds again, going, I can't drink that stuff, it gives me burning shits.

I went, Fucking everything does. Just fill me a bong.

[9]

So he did, a couple in a row from the little pile of mind-stop on the LP between his legs, the whole time flapping his jaw with those little things of foamy shit at the corners of his mouth, so that you get your fixing goggles on them and they're all you ever end up paying any attention to. But he kept on going off the whole time he was filling bongs about how these Cattle Company grocery dudes were all going to be at Chuckie Goldman's bash full force to the gills, and about the kinds of Trans Am Corvette kinds of cars these dudes cruise around in, and about how these cars are really just extensions of their penises that they use to subliminally impress the camel-toed chicks at the Cattle Company, and on and on about all this other related bogus mind-action shit from some stupid-assed psychology class he was in at the time.

I woofed down bong three and tuned right out, my mind floating off and my body feeling pulled down to the bed, with Spooge as far off as the Claw when I'm toast at home and she's blowing down the major pie sessions on me, and I'm couched and out to lunch, except with Spooge I every once in a bong session will pick up on some sentence blowing out his ass that sounds worth calling him on, like when I heard him go, I like to have sex, sort of, except for the part where you actually start to do it.

That I heard, and had to go, What in fuck's sake are you talking about?

So Spooge had to fill me in, going, *You* know, like when you're kissing with a girl, and then you're rubbing her breasts, and then you're squeezing her buttocks, and then next thing you know, you're both unzipping and fondling each other's things, and how that's all just so great and just all so much fun?

I went, Yeah, so?

So Spooge went, Well, like, then you decide to get down to the gravy and go for the goods, and so you moisten up and penetrate, and then you're in there for about a second and you blow your wad right off and you get all depressed, and your thing, your thing, you know, it goes all soft and you get all depressed, and then you just end up wondering, you wonder, what's the point to it all?

So I went, Spooge, ever stop to think that if you could just control your husker from coughing up the mayo at the drop of a hat and just get a little more stamina action in there, that then it might just become a little more enjoyable for you?

So Spooge went, Don't talk to me about stamina! I'm here beating off nightly to try to get stamina! It's completely different when there's a girl there! It sucks! Stamina doesn't even come into play! I could beat off forever, but if a girl's there, forget it! Stamina's out the window! I know what I'm talking about!

So I went, Spooge, there's no way you can know what you're talking about, because you're sitting here in your fucking undies and you're not talking about jack, except maybe that you like boxing your clown more than you like having sessions.

So Spooge went, Well, maybe I do! I happen to enjoy it, okay? Big deal!

So I went, Cut this shit, dude. I can deal on your always talking about eating rats, and I can deal on your penis-extension talk, but when you start going off about boxing your clown, I'm sorry, I don't think I can deal, all right?

Spooge got all huffy-puffy at that, going, Oh, I see! So

you're trying to tell me that you don't masturbate, is that it? Or is it that you just can't handle the fact that I'm more enlightened than you and willing to admit it, while you just sit there all repressed and pretend like it isn't true.

He gave me this I-just-cashed-you-under-the-table-with-my-genius-mind smile then, like he'd just beat the shit out of me at thumb wrestling or something.

So I went, I'm not pretending jackshit. I just don't want to hear about it. Far as I'm concerned, if you shake it more than three times, you're playing with it, and you can keep it to yourself.

Spooge went, Are you trying to tell me you don't? Anybody who says they don't is a liar.

So I went, And anybody who talks about it all day long is a fucking butt pirate.

Don't go thinking I'm out of bounds here, because you haven't heard some of the fucking brutal shit Spooge thinks makes him enlightened, because he's flapping his jaw to me about it, shit I not only wouldn't do, but shit I sure as fuck wouldn't be going off at the mouth about if I had.

Like check this one out: when Spooge decided to share with me about the time when he was cruising to class in his units' car on the expressway, and he unzipped and whipped out his husker right there while he was driving and started shaking hands with the fucking thing. He was telling me it was pretty intense, until he started getting all wigged out that a truck was going to come cruising alongside him, and that the truck-driver dude was going to look down and see Spooge hanging there and boxing his clown like a banshee, and think he was a turd burglar and run him off the road.

That's the exact type of thing that gets me calling Spooge a butt pirate, and then that's the exact type of thing that gets Spooge acting like he's all hurt feelings and shit, like he did when I called him one, and so I had to go, Spooge, listen. Don't be such a weenis. We both know we're five-star generals in the celibate army, and we both got our problems, but at least I don't go around talking about boxing my clown the whole fucking day. Now, if you want to box it, go ahead, box it, just don't expect me to sit around here and listen about it. Now, would you get fucking dressed? I want to book.

Spooge just hung there for a while rubbing the mind-stop on the LP between his fingers, while I had a visit with Jack, and then he got up and started changing shirts a shitload of times, because he said he was afraid everything he was putting on was going to make him break out into a rash, and when he was done with that and dressed, we booked down the dark stairs and into the dark kitchen, where Spooge put on his coat. The Potato still had her seat there at the table, torching up a match to light a fresh square, and the light from it made her face all fucked-up shadows and shit, like she was someone we didn't know, as we slipped out the door and she went, Going somewhere? as she blew out the match and we shut the door behind us and headed for the Old Man's penis extension parked there in the driveway.

[1 0]

We got in, sucked down by the furry bucket seats, and I popped the engine and booked us backward out the driveway and drove to Family Liquors, where we dropped our two twelvers of Coors on the counter while the purple-faced dude standing behind it stood there with his fixing goggles on Spooge's ID, trying to blow us pies by telling us it was fake, which it was, with the name and dates and all the vitals for Bruno Pasquarelli, and the picture pure Spooge, looking like anything but a Pasquarelli, hanging there in the picture with his vicious bottle mouth, while the purple-faced dude behind the counter was looking at it and going, You don't look Eye-talian to me. I don't know about this. I know of that Pasquarelli Construction family, and you don't look nothing like them.

So Spooge put on his wading boots and went, Listen, I know, okay? Don't rub it in. If you have to know, I don't look

Italian because of the fact that I was adopted. You had to know. Satisfied?

The purple-faced dude turned purpler and went, Sorry, and rung them up, and we booked with them out to the Old Man's car with the EAT OUT plates, and cruised out to the boonie factors, where all the condos are, where this bash Chuckie Goldman was supposed to be having was supposed to be.

We tore through four Coors each just looking for the thing, because it was all the way out there in butt-fuck land, where nothing's been developed but the streets, everything's just empty lots with FOR SALE signs stabbed in them and sometimes frames of houses that will all be put up looking just like every other one, and there's not even any grass laid down on the ground. It's nothing like behind us, where me and Spooge live, where it's all a lot older and the trees are all jumbo and the houses all look different, and where it's still sucking wind but heaven compared to out here in the boonies, where it's all empty parts of road stretching out between little plopped-down condos that Pasquarelli Construction is busy putting up in the middle of cornfields, but mostly just the blackness and the road cooking under the headlights, which I kept popping off to float through it all in the vacuum-packed no noise of the Old Man's car, while Spooge would freak, make me turn them back on again, bumming that I wouldn't let him crank any tunes.

If he wasn't hanging shotgun, I'd have cashed the fuckers permanently, cruised along without jackshit in sight until the outline of this black road showed itself to me in the dark orange light glowing down from the sky of the city behind me. I would have floated like that, not hearing a sound, not Spooge's talking on the shotgun side, flapping away while I un-huh-ed and yeah-ed just to be social, while the rest of me took off, just took off, really, thinking nothing special and just holding that wheel.

But then Spooge was pointing right across my face to this

huge sign in black and white that said, EVERGREEN, A PAS-
QUARELLI CONSTRUCTION DEVELOPMENT PROJECT, and behind it,
far off, a dark clump of condos.

Spooge went, This is them, Evergreen. Hang a louie up
there, and then you hang a ralph.

We cruised into this wide-open parking-lot type of thing,
and by then I could see that these Evergreen condo things
were just like any other condo things Bruno's old man or
anybody else's old man was having put up all over these empty
places way out here where nothing is. Just phone lines and
dinky trees stuffed in piles of dirt surrounded by just-unrolled
grass surrounding these shitloads of exactly the same painted
gray things all jammed together in groups and joined at the
walls like there's not room out here enough to even keep them
separate.

I went, How the fuck're you supposed to tell your place
from anybody else's?

Spooge looked at me like I was autistic and went, They've
got *numbers*.

Then he was pointing across my face again to this one
bunch of condo things where there were all these Trans Am
T-Tops and Corvettes and all other kinds of penis extensions
parked outside of, and I knew I was in the right place when I
saw Chuckie Goldman's big black van with the bubble windows
in back. There was an open space next to it, so I took it and
cashed the engine, and then me and Spooge just hung there
and didn't say a word, with those condo things surrounding us
like a big humongous horseshoe. I swear I felt just like that one
dude in that one joke where he's in someplace somewhere like
hell and he has to look inside all these doors to pick which
thing inside one it is he wants to get sucked into doing for the
rest of all time, and all that forever kind of shit. So there's this
dude, going through all these doors with all this unsuitable
shit going on behind them, like gruesome fat chicks sitting on
your face, or your toenails getting ripped out in slow motion,
or fist-fucking, or whatever it is, I'll leave it up to you, because

it's all ruthless, until he comes to the last door, where he sees a bunch of dudes standing knee-deep in big fat turds, and even though it might sound brutal, compared to all the other things behind all the other doors, what's behind this last one seems at least *kind* of suitable, so he goes for it. Thing is, once he's inside and the door's shut behind him, he hears this loud-assed whistle blowing and this loud-assed voice shouting, Okay, everybody, coffee break's over! Back on your heads!

I figured Spooge must've felt about the same way, because he went, This is pretty depressing shit.

I went, That's not the word. I don't even think we should bother.

Spooge popped a Coors and went, What else do you suggest? The Cattle Company? If that's what you're thinking, drop me off at home, because I'd rather be beating off.

I went, Don't start, Spooge.

Then I popped a Coors of my own and we just sat there, steaming up the inside of the windshield with our breath.

Finally Spooge went, Let's do up some more doobage. I need to be more baked if I'm going to go in there.

I went, Casual by me.

[1 1]

So we did up the doobage and slammed down our beers, and that seemed to do it, so we took our two twelvers and got out and locked up and headed for the door with the big number 7, which when we got there we stood outside of and listened to the music and voices coming from inside, and I was thinking how I'd rather be tossing meat around at the Old Man's Sizzler, or listening to the Claw blowing her rag, anything else but right there and right then. I was about to go, Let's book, to Spooge, too, when he made what you might call a decision by knocking on the door. Next thing was this voice coming closer to the other side while I looked down, watching the knob turning and pulling away, leaving me with my fixing goggles on a black T-shirt with a white iron-on of the burning Hindenburg and the big red words LED ZEPPELIN underneath.

Then there was this big raspy-lunger voice that went, Robbie?

I looked up, and there was this huge dude a head or two huger than me, holding out his hand that wasn't holding his twelver. He had pizza face severely and a laid-out-flat type of boxer nose, and except for the fact that he'd gotten much huger and had taken to dressing like the old type of burnout, he looked just like my buddy from Infant Jesus of Prague, my good old best buddy, Roy.

I went, Roy?

Roy went, Fuckin' Robbie dude man! holding out his huge hand for me to shake, and I did. I looked down and saw my hand there in his and felt like a dinky little dude, like my old best buddy, Roy, was going to lift my little hand and my whole body attached to it, shake my hand so I'd cook up into the air, and whip back down fast, cracking cement and shooting underground like a dude in a cartoon, or maybe just rip my whole fucking arm off right at the shoulder altogether.

He then did the same routine with Spooge, going, Spooge man! Good to see you! Good to see both you two dudes! Come on inside!

He walked in, and we walked in and shut the door behind us. Roy was already cutting through the crowd toward the back of the room, and me and Spooge cruised along behind him. This room was packed with the ex-burnout grocery dudes, all ironed and blow-dried and dancing to this Cattle Company tortured-elf disco shit, with their mall-rat cosmetology-school dropout girlfriends with the flared-back-hair syndrome and the camel-toe pants, and it seemed to me like Roy cruising up in front of us with his twelver in one hand was the only dude left in the black concert T-shirt and the frayed-at-the-heels bell-bottoms. Roy up ahead of us looked like one of those Cro-Magnon dudes, with those big-mother dinosaur-bone exhibit bones, and fucking tall, like his head was above the crowd as he cruised through, heading for the back of the room, going through a darkened door there. We followed, cut through the crowd, and went through it, too, and there we were in Chuckie Goldman's garage with the lights out, except for the light coming in from the room we were just in, and except for the lights from the glowing tips of squares and doobage, smokables strong-smelling with the garage door closed, the orange tips moving around shapes in the dark, dudes standing smoking with their twelvers at their feet.

Roy was standing right inside the door, smiling and going, Thought you dudes'd wanna come back here where the weed is going around.

I went, You thought right, dude. Thanks.

Spooge scoped the scene for a second and turned to Roy and went, You seen Chuckie around back here?

Roy went, Sure thing, dude. He's right over there. Follow me.

We followed Roy over to where these two dudes were standing, where it was too dark to make out their faces, when one of the dudes torched up his lighter to fire up some doobage rolled like a stogie that the other dude was holding, and in the flame from the lighter we could see that the dude who was stoking on the doobage was the dude who Spooge was looking for.

He saw us, too, and went, You dudes are right on time. I'm firing up some of these primo California buds I got in today for the very first time.

Me and Spooge and Roy put our twelvers on the floor and popped one each. Chuckie took a drag and passed it to the other dude, who took a drag and passed it on to Roy, who took a drag and passed it on to me, and it went around the bases like that until it was roached, with none of us talking and lung-blowing coughs. This shit was mind-stop in capital letters, and I was way beyond the valley, with my cheeks fluttering in the wind, while Chuckie Goldman and Spooge went off about what primo bud action the shit we smoked sure was, and

Spooge asking what it cost to take some off his hands and then bumming on the price, with Chuckie Goldman going, Shit walks, money talks, and then those two and the dude I didn't know wandering off to do bongs and leaving me the toast bandit I was with three Coors left and one in hand in that dark garage with my old best buddy, Roy Spitzig, hanging there next to me with a beer in his hand, too, not saying anything, and me not saying anything either for I don't know how long, until I took a square out and Roy went, Bum a smoke off you, dude?

After I gave him one and torched them both, and we were just standing there smoking, I all of a fucked-up sudden got this fucked-up idea in my head, this idea in my fucked-up head about Roy there. And it was even though I hadn't even seen the dude since seventh grade when him and me weren't buddies anymore, when Roy was the bad dude of Infant Jesus of Prague, that dude who smoked and spit and swore, that dirty-looking dude with the mean-looking pizza face who never wore his clip-on or combed his hair, that dude who the Claw called the Pagan Baby, with the mom in the kidney machine and the seven no-good brothers, all ex-Marines, and it was even though all that shit, I still got this fucked-up idea in my head that Roy had something important that it was important for him to tell me, and I didn't even have a shit's clue what. Not tossing meat or pumping gas or bagging groceries, but maybe something that Roy had to say, maybe just Roy saying something important.

I took out my one-quarter-full bottle of Jack and held it out. I held it out in the dark in the direction of Roy and went, Here. I want you to take this. Have it. It's yours.

He reached for it and took it, and went to me, Thanks.

I watched him unscrew it and have a long visit, cashing his beer as a chaser and copping a fresh one from the twelver at his feet. The Jack was almost gone.

I went, Roy?

Roy went, Yeah?

I went, I want to ask you something. That okay?

Roy went, Piece of cake.

I went, I don't really know what I want to ask, just, like, not stupid shit. Something maybe important.

Roy went, Shoot.

I went, I don't know. You've been around here since you've been born, right? Lived here your whole life and shit?

Roy went, Fuckin'-A, dude.

I went, Right, so you know what it can be like, what it gets like when it feels like everything's crawling right up your ass and won't come back down. What are you supposed to do when that happens, you know? What the fuck're you supposed to do?

Roy laughed raspy and took a tug off his beer and went, Fuckin' dude, you tell me, right? He laughed again. He went, Fuckin' you tell me.

I went, Roy, if I could tell you, I wouldn't be asking you.

Roy stood there for a minute and then went, You wanna know what I think, huh?

Roy went, You really wanna know, I'll tell you. Listen. Check this out. Like my one brother. Fuckin' my brother, man, happen you're my brother and you get married and you have two kids like him. My brother's two kids? Check it out, they both came out retarded, *both* of them, fuckin' *both* retarded, and the ugly kind of retarded, too. Happen that's you. What do you do? Or happen you're my *other* fuckin' brother and half your fuckin' foot gets blowed off in the Marines. You ain't got no foot. What the fuck do you do?

Roy went, What the fuck, happen you find out some chick you're fuckin' is fuckin' someone else, or happen you're out of weed and can't find none to smoke, or happen you get home late from work and everybody you know is already out and you don't know where. That's all it is, dude.

Roy went, Wait, no, no, say this. Say happen it's nice out someday so you go to Wampum Woods with some whiskey or some Mad Dog 20/20. Happen you see some fuckable chicks there. Happen you fuck a whole bunch of chicks all in one day. It's just like that. Or happen you don't wanna fuck a bunch of chicks all in one day. Happen you don't even like fuckin' chicks. That's something, too. I tell you, dude, it's all just whatever, you know?

Roy tossed down the rest of the Jack and put the empty bottle on the floor next to his twelver, and I finished a Coors and cashed my square with my shoe. I copped a fresh one from the twelver at my feet and popped it open and swallowed some down.

Roy went, I really gotta take a major piss.

I went, Don't let me stop you.

Roy went, Cool. Take it easy, dude. He picked up his twelver and patted me on the arm and went, Lighten up, dude. Take it light. Nothin' ain't that heavy.

Then he booked out of the garage, taking his twelver with him, and I just hung there looking at all the dark shapes of dudes and the orange glowing from their smokables, and I knew right then it was time to be booking, but I kept on hanging there still, to kill off my beers and smoke some more squares, and when I was done and left that dark garage through that lighted door and started cruising through that crowd in that other room, I couldn't find Spooge until I talked to Chuckie Goldman, who said he did one too many bongs of that mind-stop we'd been smoking, and his eyes went up in his head and he booked outside to breathe some air.

[1 2]

I took it outside to find him and shut the door behind me. I couldn't see Spooge around anywhere, but I sort of heard this far-off goober cough splashing noise like the sound of someone yacking, so I headed for where I heard it in the direction of the Old Man's car, which was where I found him, against Chuckie Goldman's big black van, bent over, hacking and hockering over a pile of his pies.

I went, Spooge, you okay, dude?

Spooge stayed bent over but went, Yeah. He hacked and hockered a little bit more and then stood himself slow until he was standing straight up. He was looking blue and sweaty, with his hair all damp at the edges and stuck to his face. He went, Oh, Jesus, I think I'm finished. I think that doobage was dusted.

I unlocked the shotgun side and went, I hope you can make it home without yacking on the dashboard.

Spooge sawed wood the whole way home, while I tried my hardest to keep my fixing goggles on the black road cooking under the headlights, and to keep my fists on the wheel at ten and two, and to keep my foot on the gas until we hit Spooge's driveway, where I threw it in park and shook Spooge to wake him, going, You're home, dude. You're home.

Spooge grunted and squinted at me like he didn't have a shit's clue who I was, and then he went, Oh.

I went, See you tomorrow.

He went, Tomorrow?

I went, Tomorrow.

He sat nodding like he understood. Then he stopped and stared up his driveway. I hung out, waiting for him to do something, but he never did, so I reached across him and popped the door open for him. Eventually he dropped his feet out to the ground and crawled out and stood up.

He went, Later.

I went, Later.

Spooge shut the door behind him and just stood there squinting into the headlights as I booked backward and the beams shot up into his face. He lifted his arm up to shield the light from his eyes, and in that last second before the lights turned out onto the street, he looked like he would stay like that forever, like a dude breaking free from prison and getting blinded by the searchlight with no fucking place left to go to anymore.

But then the headlights left him behind there as they turned out onto the road, and that quiet-assed car cruised me

up and around that curving road, around and surrounding
Infant Jesus of Prague, back all the way to the back behind
Spooge's house, back by the bike racks and the basketball
poles. I stopped the car and parked it, without my thinking
why, and I climbed out and jumped those bike racks and
headed for those swings.

[1 3]

Infant Jesus of Prague was a huge deserted shadowy
shape, pressed up tight against the black and orange of the sky.
I had my seat on the middle swing and looked up at it, at that
school of mine that would be torn to the ground soon, and I
put my hands upon those cold rusty chains, hanging in tight
with my ass in the sling, starting off swinging and pushing back
on dirt with my feet, coming back, legs lifted, until picking up
on speed, the chains digging rust in my fingers as I tugged,
laying back into it and kicking up hard, breathing like the
rhythm in the pumping down the poles, tucking under forward
before cooking backward fast, like I was going to die if this
wasn't what I did, cold out but sweating, the creaking up the
chains, my hard exhale at that hang on the backstroke, kicked
back forward into a shoot back down.

This was swinging to shoot off like slingshot, and slingshot
is what I intended to be, so I shut my eyes tight during a sharp
swing backward, to be shot like a stone up and over that
school, and on that fast-throwing down-up-forward, I let go of
the chains and put my hands to the dark, and I let go blind off
and into the air.

[1 4]

I crack my eyes open to my body gone tiny, dressed up
neat in my Catholic school clothes, in my stiff plaid clip-on and
my bright red blazer, shiny black dress shoes on my dinky little
feet. Infant Jesus of Prague is far down there below me, that
building brick-red and shining in the sunlight. My little hand
is being held, in a hand warm and pinkish, in a hand much

bigger and older than mine is. And it's lifting me up here, up to up above here, and I'm shivers and weightless and lifting through sky, a sky sunny-blue, stretching big up above us, me and this hand holding, lifting, me here. But then the hand lets me go, and floats up off above me, and I can see a shape in black flapping robes against the wind.

It shoots up high against the bright blue sky above me, its black boots kicking air out from underneath black folds. I am floating up and following, cruising quietly behind it. This face is pink and pretty, these eyes are bright and kind, this voice is calling out to guide me, Come along with me now, my children! Come along with me now, my dears! **Q**

Better Times

I am the fool who got everybody interested in the graveyard again. Until twenty years ago, it had been the burying place of my family, then it filled up, and we started putting our people in the town cemetery, where somebody would tend the graves. I was sixteen when that happened, and I had not seen the place again until a day in early spring of last year. I was home for a visit and thought up the graveyard as a way of getting out of the house for a while.

It's way out close to the county line. To find out how to get there, I asked my grandmother. She lives with my parents and is my mother's mother. None of her blood kin are buried in this graveyard, but it is in my grandmother's nature to keep up with anything that she thinks might get forgotten, and she likes it when, after a time, people do the right thing. She likes to see right prevail, but she enjoys as well her great pleasure, which is pointing out how long it takes. When I asked her the way to the graveyard, she raised her hands and looked up as though heaven was the kitchen ceiling, and she said she was glad somebody was finally taking an interest in the place. Her directions were not easy to follow. The turns she had marked in her mind by old home places of people she had known when she was young. The roads I would need she had named herself, according to what churches were on them or what creeks their bridges crossed. But the start was clear, and I understood it.

"Take the road to Macala, and when you get to the first right, turn right right there," she said.

I drove up the path as far as I could, then I had to stop the car and walk the rest of the way.

The graveyard was overgrown—a tangle of blackberry

brambles and knee-high in broom straw. The rusted iron gate, having been left open a long time ago, could not be closed. A pine tree had grown up by the gate, and the post and hinges had become a part of the tree trunk. There were thorny, dried vines hanging in the trees and twisted along the fence like barbed wire. It was a big graveyard, bigger than most family cemeteries down there. There were lots of graves, but having no new graves, it looked as if people had stopped dying. Being so grown over, it looked as if they had stopped living as well. It was quiet and so peaceful there. I went in and, picking my way around the briers and sweet-gum saplings, read every stone that had anything on it to read. The oldest graves closest to the center were marked by only plain granite stobs put there at a time when people built a box, dug a grave, and put their dead in their own ground. There were no names and dates on these markers. The mourners and rememberers of these long dead could not read or write was why. And weather over time had worn away the inscriptions on other stones. I would say later how calm I thought these dead rested, being unremembered, alone and unnamed. But all around the center of the plot, where the forgotten lay, were proper tombstones and memorials with dates and names and sweet epitaphs chiseled into the marble and granite slabs. And beyond these lay the ones who had recorded the first dates, composed the first epitaphs. Pressed up against the rusty iron fence that held in the dead, held in the vines, held in the trees planned and random, were the most recent graves. Then the fence, waist-high, forming a tight belt around the budding-up vines and trees. Scattered sprays of narcissus bloomed up against some of the gravestones and in between the tines of the fence. Tufts of new grass and wild onion grew in between the wickets.

Surrounding the graveyard was a field, about twenty acres maybe, dun-colored, a mixture of clay and powdery sand, harrowed-smooth in preparation for planting. The graveyard there so full of growth and the barren field, lifeless as though all the nutrients had been drawn from it by the wild vines and trees—it was a place that, having been forgotten by those who should have cared for it, simply suited itself.

I sat down on a stone bench that was by one of the graves. A breeze marbled the leftover winter cold with new warm air. Then the breeze stopped, and the sun felt good on the side of my face. The sky was so clear, and the air light with the scent of tender green and wormy earth. So quiet. Not a ripple in sight. I lay down on the bench and fell asleep and did not dream.

A door slammed and woke me up. On the front porch of the house across the path, a woman stood. I waved and she waved back. Then she came off the porch and started walking toward me. She walked fast, as though she were going to chase off a stray dog. When she got to the fence she stopped, and I stood up. I always behave in a fine way around people who wouldn't know fine ways. It is a flaw in me. I don't do it for the right reasons. And it is no less a flaw just because I know I do it.

"Hey," she said.

"Good morning," I said.

"Hey," she said again.

She looked to be in her fifties. Her hair was short and black and had been recently fixed in an outdated style—curled, ratted a bit, then smoothed out and sprayed. She wore glasses with silver rims around the bottoms of the lenses and two slashes of black plastic above that looked like over-made-up eyebrows. It was a Baptist face, a Primitive Baptist face—hard and holy. She was wearing a pantsuit in a blue color like no blue she would ever see in natural things, and a white blouse that buttoned up the front and was printed with mailboxes on posts. A few sprigs of grass sprouted around the posts, and bluebirds were perched on the mailboxes. Two little musical notes were balanced on the end of each bluebird's beak.

"You going to clean that place off?" she asked.

"Beg your pardon?" I asked.

She folded her arms and nodded toward the graveyard. "You going to clean that place off?" she asked again. "I love to see people look after dead folks' graves."

"I'm here for a visit," I said. "I don't live here." She walked over to a clump of narcissus growing by the gate, leaned forward, and lifted her head so as to examine the flowers through the strong part of her glasses. "Somebody ought to clean this place off," she said. She bent over from her waist and started pulling weeds from around the narcissus. I watched her arms dance around the plant.

"Well, I would, but I don't live here. And I think the place has a kind of charm, actually," I said.

"Not to me," she said. She straightened up, holding a handful of weeds she had pulled. Then she knocked the roots against the fence to clean off the dirt and put the weeds on the end of the stone bench. "It wouldn't be so bad if somebody got right on it before it grows up good-fashioned."

I said nothing and sat back down on the bench. She stood by the gate and looked out across the empty field. "I *love* to see people look after dead folks' graves," she said again.

"I might," I said. "Sometime."

"I hope you will," she said, and she pushed against the gate, trying to close it. It did not close, but one of the iron tines came off in her hand. She shook her head slowly and said, "Lord 'a mercy," as though really to say what a sorry mess, nothing sadder. We looked at each other for a moment. I expected an apology, but she made none. Then, from the house, someone hollered "Estelle!"

I looked and saw a man standing in the doorway, holding open the screen. "Your cabbages is boiling over," he yelled.

"Well, turn down the heat!" she yelled back. She leaned the piece she had broken off against the gate and started back toward the house, got only a few feet and turned, studied the thing she had broken, and came back to the gate. "Can I have that thing?" she asked.

"Yes, take it," I said.

She took it and went off down the path. I watched her until
she got to her yard, pushed the piece of fence into the ground
beside a sapling, and tied together the rod and the tree with
a piece of string she took from her pocket. The man had been
holding open the screen door ever since he had called her, and
he held it still while she climbed the porch steps and walked
past him into the house. I saw the door swing shut behind her,
and in two seconds heard it slap to. I sat for a little longer on
the bench, then I went out of the graveyard, walked down the
path to where I had left my father's car, and drove back home.

"I told them all, every last one of them, that it had to
be done," Grandmother said, taking a plate of food that she
had put aside for me from the oven. "Told them it just
couldn't wait. Now is the time, I said, before everything buds
up and starts to sprout and it gets snaky down there." She put
the food on the table in front of me: two fried chicken legs,
shriveled like water-soaked fingers, some boiled string beans,
and a mound of mashed potatoes, crusted over like old snow.
She poured a glass of iced tea and sat it by my plate. Then she
went to the other end of the table, where she had a towel laid
out and the iron plugged into the light cord that dangled from
the ceiling. She has ironed in this way as long as I can remember, preferring it to "dragging down the ironing board," as
she says. From a brown paper bag, wrinkled and fuzzy with
use, filled with a tangle of colors, she pulled, hand over hand
like the magician's trick with the endless scarf, a ribbon of
organdy cloth. It was twisted and crepey and knotted.

"We could burn it off, see," she said, picking the knots
loose. "All the dead grass and briers and broom straw. On a
Saturday." She finished untangling the ribbon, hung it around
her neck, and went to the sink. She got the spray starch from
the cabinet under the sink, then she came back to the table
and, with her free hand, turned the iron up. The light dimmed
and three seconds were ticked off somewhere inside the iron.
She put one end of the ribbon onto the towel and, separating

the wrinkles with her fingers, sprayed the ribbon with the starch. She pressed the iron down on the material. The hot metal on the wet organdy made a sound like a cat sneezing. When she lifted the iron again, the end of the ribbon was splayed out flat against the towel, showing its colors and design—a crisp stripe of each kind in a rainbow. She peeled away the part she had done and moved up another length as long as the iron was wide.

"And what else I said was that it was a disgrace the way it is right now. What did they think the other people think? The ones that live across from it? I asked them. Their yard and fields looking like just the right way to have a yard and fields. And *that* flopped down in the middle of it." She pushed her glasses up from the end of her nose with the back of her wrist. "It reflects," she said. "Don't think it don't."

Such a thing so small as pushing up her glasses changed her face, and though not made to look younger, her face was lifted, surer, sure, as sure as she was sure of what she had said, as sure as starch, ironed.

I drank down what was left of my tea, then took the glass and plate and silverware to the sink. I started to leave the kitchen and go out to the porch to sit and swing and wait to see how long it could be that nothing would happen. But before I went, I kissed my grandmother on the cheek and smelled powder and menthol, and let the smell and that face hold me there in the kitchen. I got as far as the kitchen door, though, before I let myself stay. Then I turned around and leaned on the doorjamb and thought, Let's do it, let's see who knows what.

"Why does it reflect, if it does?" I asked her. "Why does it?"

She rolled up the organdy ribbon that she had finished ironing, put a rubber band around it, and placed it in a fresh paper bag taken from the supply of fresh paper bags she kept in the kitchen safe. Then, from the old bag, she took another ribbon, purple moiré. "That is not any kind of a question," she said, turning the iron down to a cooler setting for the moiré. "If you have a question, it is this. Do you care?"

"I would if I thought it did," I said.

She put one end of the purple ribbon onto the towel and pressed the iron down on it. Then she pulled the remaining length of ribbon under the iron with a graceful flourish, drawing her arm back and out as though raising it to strike. The ribbon, creased and wrung, slithered from one side of the table, under the iron, then raced out from under the other side, shiny and flat, until the whole length of it flipped into the air over her head, then floated back to the table like a trail of descending purple smoke.

"What you think won't change what I know," she said. "And besides, you've got it wrong and backward. You've got to care first." She put the purple ribbon away and reached deep into the old bag, up to her elbow, without looking. She brought out a red ribbon of real satin. "Isn't this pretty?" she asked. "It's from a time before they started making them from acetate. And such a pretty color. The florists call it Better Times." She started working on the red ribbon, doling it out onto the towel, straightening and pressing, the iron releasing a steamy, starchy smell and the smoothed ribbon inching its way across the table toward me. Then, when she had ironed about two feet of ribbon, a glue stain in the shape of a curly-handled H appeared. The light from the bare bulb above caught in some specks of silver glitter that were still embedded in the weave of stained satin where the glue had been, and as she ironed, more faint, light-dusted letters came out. U, then S, on and on until a whole word lay on the table between us, and the word was HUSBAND. When she had finished she took the ribbon up, holding it out in front of her, letting lengths of it fall over the back of each hand in the manner that a priest holds the stole out to them before he ties together the hands of the bride and groom. **Q**

The Last Man on Earth

My aunt would say that my sisters were three wills willed of the same bent willow, mad-bent against the world like their mother, against God and a good person's reason, a switch broom of wild hair in place of a straight answer that my sisters were but leaf and stem of, with the same hang of wild knots strung together to make a Jesus weep, my aunt would say, and that we would all see whose branch would break first and willow-weep most when my father's face was the one to snap back to, and that the twig switch set on top of the refrigerator was just that reminder, a needle pointing in the direction that these things were all going to take—whatever things they were that time that my sisters had said or done to bend her branch the wrong way, my aunt said, the wrong way to the side of commotion for young girls to take upon themselves in the face of a provider, to take up into their smart heads and out onto their switch-forgetful tongues, like a quiver of arrows sent switching against her, my aunt would say, instead of just doing the thing said, the thing least expected in return to the provider, the sweeping of the home place clean, or maybe if not the iron, then the fold-and-put-away, stacked-up-even of the clothes of the man who brings home the dinner and the flapped-back shut into the wall of the ironing board on the porch, as asked, as a least thing expected, instead of a switch broom tossed back in the very rooms provided, by some one or other of my sisters, like a self-willed wicked standing willow, my aunt would say, bent on splitting wild hairs against any brisk wind and God.

Whenever the twig switch on top of the refrigerator upstairs was somehow bent the wrong way to the side of commotion, with the pointy end sticking out over the cake cover, or whenever my aunt found the switch in the toilet bowl, broken up into a handful of stick fingers that wouldn't flush, we would watch my aunt get my uncle's wood-handled wing shears from the garage and snap down another twig from one of the fruit trees, just in case the first switch broke, so that my aunt could always go back and get the twin brother, we thought, or maybe snap the one this time shot out the little greener and likelier to bend, not break into nubbed stick-fingers for my aunt to wet-pinch out of the bowl of the toilet.

We would watch my aunt walk under the fruit trees with the long-handled shears from the porch window or from behind the low, big-iron-bed bedroom window, looking for a branch that was the right thin-enough and long-enough for three girls to live with and a young tree to live without, we thought, going back and forth under the trees until she found the one it would be nothing to cry about to cut, and then my sisters would say that my aunt had her black finger back, her black finger back on top of everything, just waiting to point at the who-to-blame-most.

When my aunt had the new black finger up on top of the cake cover with a "We'll see how the bough bends," or the maybe two fingers up there this time, together, like the big and little hands of a cake-cover clock, both skinny points pointing to the same, somewhere-out-there unlucky number, my sisters would send me up into the kitchen upstairs where my aunt lived, to see how long what was up there was, how pointy-out over the refrigerator, and if my aunt had left any of the hard nubs on.

I would climb then up onto the plastic-covered kitchen chair nearest the refrigerator to look and see, and maybe even to touch, for my sisters, and my aunt would tell me it would be best for me to just stay out of the wind, out of this wind entirely, out of the direction this wind was going to take tonight when my father would come home to put a few stray arrows back into their proper quiver.

In the time before my father came home, the long waiting time before dinner, I would tell my sisters what I could tell from just only having to look and guess and having to stay my stay-away-entirely, and my sisters would do the things that they said were things you could do to keep that black finger at a distance and keep the nubs from cutting in, in places that things, my sisters would always tell me, were not supposed ever to touch the anywhere-near-the-nub part of on a girl, or on any woman either.

In that time, I would go into the bedroom and watch my sisters put on more panties than just one pair, and then pull on the bottoms to their fluffy, wishing-wells-and-buckets pajamas, and then roll the wishing wells and buckets all up their legs and under their skirts and put on the kind of sweater that buttons up in front, and then my sisters would send me to my father's room—to the bottom drawer in my father's small bedroom with the yellow shade half always down, to get the thick wool work socks, rolled up into what looked to me like fists, down tight in two straight rows between a few skinny-over-the-shoulder thin undershirts and some old man's kind of long underwear, stacked up neat as pancakes to the corners. And I would walk back down the hallway with fist-lumps under my shirt, shots to the ribs and to the belly, and maybe one under the belt, and I would just go in and lie down for the count on the big white bedspread and let my sisters take all the lumps, all the fists to unroll and push down flat in front underneath where it might just go, my big sister would say, where it had gone before a few times and might go again. Then my sisters would sit down on the big iron bed and put the wool socks down so that they would be just down right over any nub part, so that I would be the one to stand up and say what it looked like under a sweater if it was just buttoned up every-one up to the top. Then my sisters would tell me to go and stay away, to close the door behind and just go and stay away someplace until dinner, and after dinner and maybe even after that, to stay

away until I got to be a girl, until I got to be a girl myself sometime and had to stay and wait all day on the bed for my father.

I did my stay-away, I did my stay-away-entirely where
I could, where I could be on the porch to see my father when
he walked by the windows and stood big in the doorway of the
back garage that was the washroom for the clothes and a place
for a man to get the dirt off of himself in some way decent
before dinner, my father would say, dirt that was all on him
and on his boots, where I could see from to tell my sisters
when my father had come home, and where it was all right for
me to play Last Man at the Fort, the two-stepped-up landing
of the stairs, behind the iron grill gate off the back of the porch
room, where the rose-carpeted rest of the clunk-sounding
steps, we always said, went eighteen wrong ways up to my
aunt.

It was all right to be the Man at the Gate so long as I wasn't
the Man in the Way whenever my aunt went up or down and
so long as I didn't bing, bing the black-iron pull-thing that
opened the licorice-twist grill gate to the fort and let go with
a bing that you could hear all over the house. Or I could be
the Last Man at the Fort alive to listen, to listen to the one-
single-one that I would only ever want to listen to, that my aunt
would put for me up on top of the wood stand-up Victrola with
the no-good needle, if I would just only ask and let my aunt
do the what-she-knew-the-how part and if I would do the stay-
there-and-listen-good-like-the-white-dog part, the white dog
stuck on the inside propped-up wood cover of the stand-up
Victrola, the stay-there-and-listen-good part to the one that
was the Combined Choirs of St. Vladimir's and St. Nikodim's
that was my one-single-one that I liked, until it was the
scratches-at-the-end time to go knock on the door of the bedroom and ask if any one sister would come out just only for
a minute and turn the record over or please to take the no-
good needle off. I listened to the one that was the Combined
Choirs of St. Vladimir's and St. Nikodim's black scratched

record until no one of my sisters would come out anymore to
do the needle back, but only would come out to push the finger
handle up to Off and then go back into the bedroom and close
the door, so that I just did the Last Man at the Fort thing with
the back-and-forth of the iron-grill gate and sometimes a little
bing when the pull-thing slipped off my finger until I could
hear my father's lunch pail making another metal sound in the
driveway and I could see my father moving his little side-to-
side moving when even he was walking straight, me seeing
through the porch-door window—my father, not looking back
or even in, but walking side to side a little until he was big in
the out-back doorway of the washroom, and big like a boxer
with his arms stretched out, taking off his green-faded Army
coat and sitting down inside on the kick-boot bench against the
wall, so that that was all you could see then, after my father had
sat down—just one leg crossed over the other, showing out
from behind the left-open door—my father's khakied legs, one
leg loped over a stood-up knee, with a tiny-to-see one and two
toe-wag-around-lazy, and his back-laced-around-the-top dirt
boots looking to me like nothing that my father always said
they were, a dirt-tired pair of old dogs.

Then I would be the Man in the Way, the Last Man Alive
for my aunt coming down, and then the First Man to go and
tell about it, to just go to the bedroom door to tell my sisters
that now was almost when, just the first part before the rest,
when my sisters would have to come out and sit at the table
and watch and listen to my aunt bend the branch her way, my
aunt would always put it in front of my father, her way as to
how things were going to spring right back up to rights.

During the first part that I could see through the
porch-door window and hear the most of across the back yard,
I could see my aunt doing the telling with the pointing to my
father sitting down, with the "We'll see after," and "Who
smarts after," that would always go with the pointing down at
my father until it was finished, the first part, and I would go

then to the downstairs refrigerator to get a cold can from the bottom row and bring my father out the beer he liked to drink before he had to get the dirt off, before he undid the back-laced-around laces and pulled off the dirt boots slow and then went over to the sink to scoop the sandy-clay soap out of the yellow can, with my aunt still talking and pointing, and the cold water running for sandy-clay soap that my father scooped out, big-thumbing the yellow can set in the wire rack, and gray-muddied-up his hands with first, and then spread on up into the black swirly hair forest of each arm to a bone-naked elbow, before making the sandy-clay mud-slide, mud-run, and mud-flood-away off, both arms held up under the faucet, like a boxer waiting for his gloves, when I would watch my aunt point a last, or next-to-last, straight-shook finger down toward my father's bent-over back with a "Scrub hard, and look to where your dirt runs," and I would hear her wedge-heeled quick-walk back to the house, when I would just go stand then, outside under the fruit trees, while my father moved inside to close the door a little and took off his khaki clothes that I could only hear and not see come off, hear only the little clunk of the double-eye belt buckle part of, when my father would drop his khaki pants down onto the table inside, and I could hear then the little metal clunk sound that the steel shower made when my father stepped inside the put-up-portable shower that he and my uncle had put up to leave the dirt outside where dirt belonged, my aunt had always told my father and my uncle, and I could hear the pull-across sound of the shower curtain and the turn-on of the water sound, like a sound you could almost make in your throat, when I knew it was all right for me to go back then into the washroom to sip the foam up out of the beer can bottom, and all right for me to go to stand to just look at my father while the water was still running and the curtain was still pulled across shut—my father, moving a little side to side behind the gray-white plastic clouded curtain, and me hearing then the flat sound of something flat to falling water and then the sound like rain makes on something tin and hollow, and then the clunk sounds of a someone, or it could have been a something, I thought, when a something-you-didn't-know-what was moving up over you on top of a tin roof, before my father would turn the handle wheels of the water off and I would run back into the house to get a clean set of top-and-bottoms and a pair of fist-rolled socks out of my father's bottom drawer and run back to put them up on top of the table in the washroom and then close the door behind good, while my father dried himself off with the green, rack-hung towel, alone in the washroom, and put on his home-clothes up off from the nail board and swooshed, in his Father's Day-bought brown leather slippers, across the back yard and in to dinner.

Then would come the sit-down part, when it would some-times be just a finger-length of twig down on an empty plate in front of a sister, and my aunt not even pointing, just talking about who had the smart answer now, if anyone had the smart answer to these things before dinner, and my father would say to let's eat now, to let's just everybody eat this dinner now, to come home to without commotion, without what-all commo-tion in anybody's ear until after the dinner, until a man could sit down to a piece of bread for a minute without a tree falling down onto his plate, his plate that he had got himself clean to sit at without the commotion, my father said, and then he would tell everybody to get their plate as well clean and to take, take some first.

During the passing and the spooning and the cutting and the eating, I would put the little stick-fingers passed under the table into my pocket and my aunt would put the speckled blue roast pan or the two-ton iron stew pot in the middle of the table and say to let a hungry slave do the rest after this family, the rest after her ironing and folding and looking all after and letting her own husband wait upstairs like a field hand for his dinner, all for a bunch of wild hairs flung in her face, like a wild woman he and all here knew well of, my aunt would tell my father, for all the neighborhood to know that she, my aunt, was just a stood-up tree in her own house to be back-talked back to by a handful of skirt trying to be a dress under this one roof, and that he, my father, ought to have the at least half-breath of decent brother's breath left in him to do the least some little thing about it, about this "come from a she-wolf, be like a she-wolf" everyday slap in the face without fear nor shame in front of God or the postman.

Then my father would say that he would put the shoe on to fit right on this family after dinner, after a man could have his dinner sit in his stomach for five minutes out of the day without every passing creature come to soil on it, any stray bit of dog on the street come to take his ease on the place where a man was taking his dinner after a day's work, if it was possible for a man not given to ask much of his God to have a goddamn moment to see where the rock was in the shoe and to take care of it peace and quiet, with peace and quiet over his table. And my father would get up out of his chair, with a "Don't everybody else get up," and go out back to walk under the fruit trees in the garden, while my aunt quick-walked up the iron-gated stairs with a loud bing sound ringing all over the house, and then my father would swoosh back in a little while later, when my sisters would be already scraping plates into the garbage in the pantry, and sit down at his place at the head of the table and eat quiet while my sisters soaped up the sink-stacked rest of the dishes, and I, each by each, dried up the silver.

When it was my father, alone in the dining-room alcove after dinner, sitting in his lion-paw-knuckled oak armchair at the table listening to the tiny-bulbed hand-me-down wood radio to the news, up close so that he could hear the man's English, my father would say, and me still in the kitchen, doing my one-potato, two-potato with the spoons and the forks and the knives all to lay out even before I could close back the drawer, my sisters would do their stay-away-from-my-father-entirely back on the back porch and put on a whisper-like-only other record than the scratchy one that was the

Combined Choirs of St. Vladimir's and St. Nikodim's that was my favorite one to put on, and my sisters would sit down on the long pew bench against the wall or around the back round table with the lion claws cut deep into the wood legs at the bottom and sew into their round hoop wooden things that my aunt would give them to sew things in, and I would go into the pantry and take the stick-fingers out of my pocket and put them all under the potato peelings and other things deep that I could not see to say just what in the dark, and sometime around then, before the man with the news was all finished, I could hear my aunt quick-come down the stairs, the bing, and then the music *pik-puk* stop.

Before the man with the news was all finished, the wind and the weather would start up, the commotion that started at the top of the stairs and came down onto the back porch and on into our rooms downstairs with a weathervane of its own, along the hall and into the front room, where my father was listening close to the man's English—my aunt, holding the pointiest-one twig black finger that I could see from the doorway to the kitchen, holding the twig switch in one hand and then turning with a click and pulling off straight the little-screw-lost white knob of the wooden radio, reaching over the table in front of my father, pulling the white knob off and then putting it into her front blue button-up sweater pocket with a "If you don't, then I will."

Then my aunt would throw the switch at my father's feet, then pick it up again and put it into a quiver, shaking and looking for a one sorry among her many sorrows, my aunt would say, a one sorry that my aunt said she could not find anywhere among the three of them, anywhere at all in a talk-back house that was going to stay her house and none of it other, and my sisters would first hold up their hoop things, their hoop things with the needles still hanging down from them, and then back up like a boxer would, I thought, yes-and-no back, yes-and-no back, all the way out of the hallway, with my aunt saying, "Sorry-yes!? Sorry-yes!?" every time down with the nubby end-quivering black finger, until I could see my father stand up and take off the double-eye belt and then it was "Answer this!" and "Answer that!" and then just my sisters' arms up without any hoops and needles now, and my father's "Answer her something, just!" and all the things I could always hear when there was a commotion in the house: the flat sound of the double-eye belt against skin, the sprung-bunk sound of dropped wooden frames bent thin into circles, and the sound of the switch against just skirt when it missed bare leg or arm—all the sounds of a commotion that brought my uncle, with always a couple-of-two-good-dollars' worth of change in his home-clothes gray pants, coming down the stairs with his late-to-church clump and bing and "What's the holler?"

What the holler was was something I should just listen to and know well what was good for me, my uncle from upstairs would tell me, telling me then to just keep back out of the way of things, when the way of things was not my business to put myself in front of, when the tree stood shaken and it wasn't my tree to shake. "What's the crazy holler!?" my uncle from upstairs would say to the ones who were hollering still. "What's crazy about to high-holler in the house?!"

The holler in the house that my uncle said was crazy-odd-lunatic to put in the ear of a neighbor, in the ear of the whole neighborhood, was just one more holler that I could hear on the back porch, the last back room, where my sisters would go to get away from the black finger and the double-eye belt, in the corner by the porch window, where my big sister would pull down at the flap-down ironing board and stand with the other two sisters like a shaken sister-tree just behind—what was half pulled-down and half slid-fallen out to a dead-end stop, flat to ceiling and floor, like the hard clap of the wing of the Last-Minute Always-There Angel, who could wing down out of pure air anytime and put an angel wing through even a wall, my aunt would tell me, sharp and fast and hard as the quick of an arrow, without an arrow's afterward thin quick quiver, but hard down-falling as the wing bone of the cross, my aunt said—what I thought from what I could see from behind the twist-iron gate and hear holler and screech of in my ears— my upstairs uncle doing the hollering now with the rest and grabbing at the flapping tongue of my father's double-eye belt, yelling at my sisters, "Don't raise your arms to my face! Show you to raise an arm where it don't belong!"

Then my uncle from upstairs would grab the twig switch from my aunt, because my father said the double-eye belt was but his godforsaken business to buckle up any hell down here and his goddamn pants up both with, and then my uncle would say that he was going to show my sisters now what belonged, what belonged and what didn't under his roof, and my aunt would *pik-puk* put the needle back down onto the record and fumble the finger switch over to where it had to be for the wood stand-up Victrola to start to play, and I could hear my sisters crying still over the music that was for dance-time and dilly-dally, and I could see the wishing wells and buckets fall-ing down around my youngest sister's red-looking legs, with bumps all on them, until my biggest sister would push her hair back out of her face with the backs of both hands and look straight at my father and say, "You stop it!" without crying anymore that I could see—"You stop now!" just like that to my father, and my father would unroll his fist-wrapped-around double-eye belt and throw it like a snake into the corner by the porch door and say he would kill God out of anyone that touched it before he did, including my aunt and my uncle, and any man on God's earth that might come walking through that door to lay another hand down on his children, and then my big sister would push the flap-down ironing board back up and take my other two sisters, arm-wrapped-around past my aunt and my uncle from upstairs, on into the big-iron-bed back bedroom just off the porch, and close the door behind good, and then my uncle would scratch the needle off the record that my aunt always told us was for dance-time and dilly-dally, and my uncle would tell my aunt then to stop the goddamn thing going before he went and backed out the Buick and rode right the hell right over it, and my father would walk then out of the back porch door, out under the fruit trees, with the yellow bug porch light flicked early to on by my Last Man Home Always upstairs uncle, the bulb already getting a few early pinch-wing moth moon-walkers under the jut roof out over the door—my father, that I could see under the trees staying his stay-away from the light—me standing, Last Man in the Doorway under the early, yellow-light-footing moonwalkers, here and there a little winged-moth moon-wink, and my aunt, moving behind me, flapping flat-shut the wall-door to the ironing board and dropping down, snap-button-good, the wood cover to the stand-up Victrola, and my uncle binging the iron gate behind him, going up, saying everybody could just go eighteen ways back to hell before he would soon bother about a damn bunch of high-holler—my father, that I could see moving under trees, with the inside bottoms of his fists raised up to his eyes, like a boxer covering up when it is all over and the referee has to step in, I thought, or maybe just even looking like the way it looked to me at church—my father looking to me then like the man who was Adam, my aunt would tell me, Adam in the high lead-vined colored-glass church window that I passed slowly by with my aunt on Sundays, going down the long aisle inside and looking at it up—up at the man who was Adam, with his fists raised up to his eyes and no tears that you could see, crying down on one knee in the corner and covering up to the light where God was, high up over the trees of the garden, because God had given the woman in the picture, my aunt would tell me, the willow of hair to weep in. **Q**

The Only Light to See By

The girl was trying to show her mother how the people down the road were found dead. The girl lay every which way on the sheets with the American Eagles all over them, saying, "This is how the daughter was found dead, and this is how the father was found dead, and this is how the mother was found dead."

The girl's mother lifted up the covers and covered the girl with them, making the bed as if the girl were not there, the mother thought to herself, as if the girl were just another American Eagle on the sheets.

The girl wanted to go down the road to the house. At first, the mother told the girl that she could not go, but then the mother told herself that if it was something the girl wanted to see, then the mother would go with the girl, and the mother thought that seeing the house where the family was actually killed might stop the girl from every once in a while, while they were eating dinner or watching television, might stop the girl from lying out on the floor in the way one of the bodies was found and saying to her mother, "Guess who I am now, the father or the daughter or the mother."

It was raining when they walked down to the house. Worms had come out from the dirt on the sides of the road and the worms stuck to the bottom of their shoes, and the girl told her mother that she had learned that you can cut a worm in half and it will still crawl.

Walking behind her mother, the girl told her mother that the back of her mother's head, where no hair grows and leaves a circle of skin, that the back of her mother's head was the moon and that the long hair that still grew down from the sides of the moon was the night.

The girl led the way to the house. She counted the worms

she killed under her shoes, saying, "Two, four, six, eight," counting double because she said she knew that when you cut a worm in half that both ends will live.

First thing the girl said to her mother was that it looked like their house. That, from the outside, the girl said, it looked as though people lived in there. Then the mother and the girl saw a dog on the porch and the girl said, "It must be the family dog, come back to the house to sit and wait for the family to come home."

The mother and the girl stood outside the ropes that circled around the house, and the girl said to her mother that it was as if they were watching a parade and the house was a float that had lost its air and now could not float any longer and had come down to the ground.

The girl told her mother that she wanted to come back to the house after the rope was gone or that she wanted to come back when it was night.

The mother took the girl back home. When the mother went to bed that night, the girl stood up on her mother's bed and wrapped the covers around herself like a cape, and the mother thought to herself that the girl looked as if she were an eagle, grown from out of the sheets and ready to fly.

In the middle of the night, the girl was gone. The mother walked down the road and called for the girl, but the mother heard no answer. When the mother reached the house where the bodies had been found dead, she went under the ropes and into the house.

The television was on and it was the only light to see by in the house. There was what the mother thought was dried blood on the floor by the couch, but because it seemed to be such a dark color in the television light, the mother thought it could have been anything on the floor and that it could have even been water.

Then the mother saw the girl lying on the couch, one arm up over her head, fitting into the line of chalk that had been drawn to show how the daughter had lain when the daughter had been killed.

The mother called to the girl, but the girl was asleep. Then the mother sat down next to the girl and put the girl's feet up on her lap, and the mother looked around the room. By the wall she saw the chalk lines where the father had lain when he had been killed. The mother looked for the other mother's place where she had been killed, but she could not find the lines of chalk. Then the mother put her arm on the couch and she saw that where she was sitting there was an outline drawn in chalk of someone who had long hair, and the hair had gone over the back of the couch, and the mother thought to herself that what it looked like was a flame reaching down to the ground, and the mother then thought that it was where she was sitting that the other mother had sat when the other mother had been killed.

The girl woke up and looked at the back of her mother's head, and the girl told her mother that she thought that it was the back of her mother's head that was lighting up the room at first, and not the light from the television. "I thought the moon was in this house," the girl said to her mother, and then the mother lifted up the girl and carried her home.

At home, the mother put the girl into the mother's own bed, with the eagles on the sheets, and the girl lay down and slept as if what she was trying to do was fit into one of the eagles, spreading her arms out like wings, and then the mother got into bed and lay on top of the girl, so that the back of the mother's head, with the circle of skin with the hair hanging down from its sides was facing up and looked like the moon, and the mother thought that if they were both to be killed in their sleep, she and the girl would be found as one, the mother on top of the daughter in a circle of light. **Q**

Caper

On my fourteenth birthday Aunt Agnes came into my room and closed the door behind her. "Enjoy the party?" she asked, sitting with a delicate twitch of her ass on the edge of my bed.

"Sure," I said.

Years before, during the last hour of another party, the one celebrating her marriage to my Uncle Feldstein, I asked her what it was she did when she was "in the business."

She was sitting in an armchair and I was cross-legged on our pale pink wall-to-wall carpet, trying to look up between her legs. My mother was standing apart at the other end of the room, and by that sense of mothers that all boys have, I knew that she was holding her breath.

"Well, Michael," Agnes said, stirring champagne with her finger, "gentlemen like yourself would call on me and we'd spend some time together. And then they'd pay me."

I was satisfied with that, my mother breathed again, and Agnes looked fresh with triumph.

The next day I told my friend Archie Winstin, "My uncle married a whore." I was proud of it, and I was proud of knowing it.

"That was great about the prize," my aunt said now, sitting next to me on my bed, in my room, which smelled of dirty socks and suddenly of drunkenness and perfume also. "Yeah, that sure was. That really was."

Agnes meant the prize I'd won for a picture I took of a man falling off a beam at a construction site. I was a creative youngster.

A lot of my pictures got published in the paper, so a prize wasn't a big deal to me then.

My aunt stood up and stripped herself; she was naked

quickly. "Don't be afraid," she said, but at my age there was nothing else to do.

She got in bed next to me (stiff as an emery board) and smoothed my hairless chest and stomach. She began by kissing my shoulders.

I came all over my stomach.

Minutes later (I'm not showing off, I was fourteen), I was inside a woman for the first time. Fantasy already played a great role in my life. She was sitting on me and I had my eyes closed, seeing the lady in the stationery store where I stole in the hope of getting caught, and the skinny woman who worked in my uncle's Photo Lab and wore pink lipstick, and the teen-age girl I had a crush on that my uncle used to go out with before he married Agnes. So maybe I was having my revenge.

I opened my eyes and stared at her breasts. "How can you carry those around?" I asked.

"You sort of get attached to them," she said.

Agnes came many times that month. She taught me to laugh in bed, and that there's no difference between giving and taking. Happy birthday.

My uncle offered me a job in his store. In the back of the Photo Lab there were five racks of expensive stolen coats. I asked Feldstein why they were there and he told me a friend left them because he didn't have room.

But I knew a lot about commerce by then. Feldstein had had me running numbers, or being his bagman. I was a big kid, and I'd worked the docks before Archie Winstin had his first paper route. (Incidentally, he made a lot of money off that route, because I showed him how to run it. There are always a lot of things you can do on the side, other people to involve; no one trusts anyone else, which is how you could turn a buck. There are two kinds of work, and mostly I did the legal kind.)

I was the only kid I knew that wasn't a dangerous little hood at heart.

About the coats. I called Frankie, a sort of wholesaler I knew, to look at them. He came after closing and offered me three grand.

"I'm not going to cut Feldstein's throat for that kind of dough," I said.

"Am I a charity organization? No, I'm a businessman."

"Then do business elsewhere, you cheap small-time crook." I had to act tough with Frankie, because he was always holding out. Especially because he thought he could walk all over me because I was just a kid.

"Okay," he said. "Since they're from out of town, I can work the insurance scam with you."

"Fine. Fifty percent for me. And not a word to Feldstein about it."

There was a noise at the back door; it was either rats or my Uncle Feldstein.

He was with two hairy, stupid-looking guys. One of them was probably going bald, also less stupid, and obviously the boss.

When Feldstein walked in, he saw me posing with a fur. "You look like a princess, now put it back."

The other guys looked annoyed, but not enough to say something. The bossy guy was snooping around the coats like the snub-nosed shark he was. The stupider guy looked like he was carrying a B-52 bomber under his jacket.

"This your friend?" I asked my uncle.

"Yeah, this is my friend."

"He's got more room now?"

"That's right. He might take them back now."

The friend turned and showed his shark teeth.

"How come his friend's carrying a gun?" I asked.

Stupider patted his left tit. Feldstein laughed.

Frankie was in a corner being invisible.

Feldstein and his friend whispered bad things to each other, sounding like two snakes fucking. Then the friend looked at Stupider, who pulled his piece. Feldstein lost his head and rushed him with his hands up like a linebacker. A shot was fired. Stupid spun around with the gun still cold in his hand, looked at Frankie in the corner, and faded out.

"Beat it," Frankie said solemnly to my uncle's pale balding friend, and he did.

Feldstein sat on the floor, useless with surprise.

Stupid was dead.

Shooting someone has to do with the business, and when I was doing a job, I didn't let it bother me if I had to do it. Later, months later sometimes, I'd remember with a vivid slow-motion clarity. I never blamed myself, but I still felt very sad. I'd punish myself by thinking of the widow an' kids, the ailing grandmudda, but I never did anything corny like send a check. I didn't even know half the guys. Some I knew.

So what does a kid like me do for the next seven years? Drop out of school, work for Feldstein, take the equivalency, quit Feldstein and go to medical college in Mexico, drop out after two years and work for Feldstein, quit again and go to the Art Students League. Feldstein, Feldstein, Feldstein, and then the scholarship. Maybe there was something in the nature of revenge for Feldstein, getting me in his line of business and not letting go.

On my twenty-first birthday, Feldstein stuck his head in the door frame of the studio. "Psst." Feldstein would never set foot in a place like that, out of respect.

He took me to the Hickory House coffee shop on 57th Street. "I could take you someplace fancy. But you can put it in your memoirs that your Uncle Feldstein took you to the lousy Hickory House."

Feldstein was always generous. He'd trusted me with everything since the deal with Frankie and the coats. He needed me, and I needed him like a hole in the head and I knew it. I'd been running from Feldstein for a long time.

"Need some dough?" he asked.

"Everything's fine," I said.

"I mean, I could give you a little job. Wouldn't take too much time."

His little jobs were never easy, but I was still living off the last one. I'd been wondering what I'd do when that ran out; I'd quit Feldstein more than a year before, for the last time, I'd said.

"I can count on you's why. It's all planned, but I still need you. It's complicated."

Habits are hard to break. He was my uncle.

"But never again."

Feldstein smiled. He'd heard that before.

It was 5 A.M. in the morning at night. Mr. Alvarado was the biggest complication so far, and he was sitting next to me in a truck stop near Palomar. He was nervous.

We had crossed the border in Southern California because it should have been easier than crossing in Texas. Alvarado wasn't Mexican, but being small and dark, he got the border guards excited anyway.

We were hauling a van full of household goods, stolen paintings, and cocaine worth ten million dollars. There were some horrible reproductions thrown in along with Mr. Laurel's genuine Goyas and Rembrandts. Alvarado's cocaine was stuffed into the frames of the fakes. All of this had been my uncle's idea.

Except for Alvarado. It was a neat idea to swing two deals at one time, but Alvarado decided he had to come along. He was a young guy, His family had a good reputation in my uncle's circle. This was his first big deal, and he was more afraid of getting ripped off by Feldstein or his buyer than he was scared of Customs and Immigration. But he was a scared kind of a guy. I wondered why his family was making him do this. Maybe it was some kind of ritual, and if you come out alive, they let you fuck some virgin. Maybe Alvarado was the virgin. I decided he was. It's just another way of categorizing people.

So a guard hassled us at the border. Nothing but routine early-morning suspicion. I told Alvarado, "He's looking for the sixteen brothers and sisters he thinks are *between* the paintings." But Alvarado was nervous and got out of the van.

The next step was meeting Mr. Laurel near Palomar and then taking both these guys to meet Feldstein and the buyers, at a farm outside San Pedro. It seemed too complicated, and I thought, I should be the one who is running this thing.

Alvarado came over and started to whisper, which is one thing not to do. It gets these guys mad. The guard checking the stuff in the back came over.

"What's all that stuffer?"

"Furniture for my new house," I said.

"Where d'ya buyum?"

"Zacapa," I said.

"Have receipts?"

I showed him, and he ordered us out of the car. He called for some help, and a bunch of boys began to dismantle the dashboard. I didn't mind so long as we weren't going to be late, but Alvarado was jumpy and the guards kept taking steady looks at him.

"Stop advertising yourself," I said.

"Maybe I should have worn a tie," he said.

"Maybe I should have worn tails and a ten-gallon hat," I said. Alvarado nodded seriously, not getting it.

While we were waiting for Laurel at the truck stop near Palomar, I ordered an egg-salad sandwich. I still had sand caught in my teeth from the drive across the desert, but food was food. I didn't care about the stuff, but you tend to let down your guard if you don't eat.

Alvarado ordered a coffee.

"You should eat," I said.

"I can't. When you can't, you can't."

There was just no telling how long we were going to have to wait for Laurel, who was already an hour late, or Feldstein, either.

"Sometimes you better eat anyhow," I said.

"When you can't, you can't," he said. We were both talking bullshit simple Latino wisdom. Short phrases that are supposed to stand for big ideas. Doesn't work that way. Half-baked.

He looked at me like I was some kind of specimen of desert-animal life. The kind that's well suited for the conditions. "I envy you," he said. "You're a natural for this business."

A tall fat man in a rough white suit creased the doorway of the truck stop. Here was trouble. I had a bad feeling for Alvarado.

"Good morning," Laurel greeted us, and I knew he'd been up for hours. Which didn't explain his being late.

We all had a copy of Feldstein's map. Giving everyone a map was unnecessary, I thought. He should have let me plan this from the start. From now on, I thought, that's the way it's going to be. Then: What the hell am I thinking about? This is the last time.

Laurel made sure it was a long ride. Leaning across Alvarado's body to chat, he forced Alvarado to push against my right arm. Steering was difficult.

"Business is great, eh, Alvarez?" he said. Cheerful like the Chamber of fucking Commerce. (You can meet a lot of tough characters hanging around there. Con men and CIA types.)

"Michael here's a painter," Laurel said. "That's a fine business to be in, eh, Alvarez?"

"Alvarado," Alvarado said.

"Ha ha. Seriously, he should stick to that. Painting's not dangerous."

"So who's afraid?" I blustered. Laurel had a strange effect. Whenever you tried to show him how tough you were, you came off looking like Winnie the Pooh in a huff. Laurel was wearing white, but he was a real tough guy, and he didn't have to let you know to let you know.

When a jeep crossed the road a few yards ahead and stopped in the middle, I knew what Laurel had been doing all morning.

I wondered if Alvarado's mother was going to get some kind of a pension. My job wasn't to protect anyone except Feldstein and the merchandise.

Alvarado asked pitifully, "What's this?"

"Probably my uncle checking up," I said.

Laurel and I got out to give his hoods a clear shot. The hoods didn't miss.

I turned to Laurel and said, "If you're planning a surprise party for me, you'll find I'm not easy to kill." Bluster, bluster.

"I have no doubt," Laurel said. Trustless confidence. I thought, He's killed his father and fucked his mother. He's fucked his sister. He's gotten it from every whore he wanted, and for nothing.

Laurel's hoods wrapped up the body before it bled too much, and we left.

Feldstein was late. We found an old campfire and started it up while we waited.

"Tell me," Laurel said, crouching but not sitting so he wouldn't dirty the seat of his pants, "why do you play these dangerous games?"

"Dangerous for who?"

He smiled. I told you the effect that kind of talk has on Laurel. "Is it money? I'm just curious. Money's a good reason. I like money. That's why I'm here. I don't trust anyone with my money."

Laurel liked listening to himself talk, and so did I. But guys who fuck their mothers are totally selfish. Guys like that take exactly what they want. Guys like that start early and they never stop protecting it.

"You have to make a choice sooner or later," he said. "One life or the other."

"What do you know about my choices?" It just seemed like one of those conversations people have while they're waiting for Feldstein and the buyers.

"You're an artist and you're playing at gangster."

"What makes you think I'm playing," I said, trying to narrow my eyes.

Laurel laughed. "I don't mean you're an amateur. I'm not saying that. But if this was your real life, I'd know everything there is to know about you. And if you do become a pro, I'll know where you sleep and who you fuck and what your little finger is thinking even before you do."

"I free-lance," I said.

"For your uncle?"

"Right."

"Blood is thicker than water?"

"Right."

This guy, I thought, isn't all that concerned with my future. He certainly wasn't dumb. Or maybe he was lucky in his choices of conversation. But he was trying to tease my mind away from . . . he's going to blow someone away. Not Feldstein. One of the buyers. Maybe he's got someone on the farm. Watch his hands, watch for a signal.

"You should stick to painting."

"Yeah?"

"Otherwise you'll get killed."

"Who'll kill me? You?"

He shrugged. "Not me."

I looked over his shoulder into the woods behind the farm.

There's an eighty-two-year-old model at the Art Students League and she's been there for sixty-one years. She's very famous because she's posed for a lot of great painters. Last month she modeled for me, and I thought she was beautiful. She models for a lot of people. What I thought while I was sitting by the fire on Feldstein's farm is that she represents continuity. Continuity seemed important. And with all these bodies, what kind of continuity could Feldstein offer?

Two cars pulled up and Feldstein got out of one of them. He had the coke buyer with him. The art buyer was alone in another car; he was a Spanish-looking guy, thin and young.

"Where's Mr. Alvarez?" Feldstein asked. He was always bad with names.

"Laurel's here instead," I said.

"But he was so anxious to be here himself, that's so . . ."

Feldstein was momentarily baffled, but not so the others. The coke dealer was petulant: So you killed him, right? The art dealer walked away.

Laurel and the coke dealer met privately, at an unfriendly impasse. Laurel was trying to raise the price.

Feldstein was trying to catch my attention, but I wasn't looking. If you look at him with his gesticulating eyebrows and glances brimming over with meaning, you're lost. I was on duty, and I also was thinking about something else—continuity.

The coke dealer wouldn't budge. "A deal's a deal."

"But your bargain wasn't with me," said Laurel.

"I didn't come all the way down here for this bullshit and I'm not going back empty."

He pulled a gun from his pocket. He had the right idea about Laurel, but he didn't have enough information. Laurel raised both hands over his head and closed one to a fist. Now I had seen the signal. A high-caliber pistol shot rang from the middle range. The coke dealer was so dead he'd never even existed.

The art dealer was more than happy to take everything off Laurel's hands. Laurel's hood dragged away the body, leaving matted weeds and a pool of blood. The bullet fired at that distance had wobbled and left a large pudding instead of a hole in a chest.

Laurel handed Feldstein five grand.

"What do you call this?"

"Your commission," Laurel said. He walked away, toward wherever men in white linen suits disappear to.

"You fucking cheap cheat," Feldstein shouted. "Stop him, will ya!" Feldstein shouted, but knowing what I did, the person I had to stop was Feldstein.

He rushed at Laurel, arms high. I should have tackled him, but I didn't. I was thinking about continuity and the eighty-two-year-old model.

Feldstein got one bullet in the lower abdominal cavity. He didn't die right off, and I cradled his head in my lap.

"You're not mad?" he asked.

"No."

"I should have let you plan it from the start."

Laurel's hood waited for the new body.

"There's a model at the school," I said. "She's been there sixty-one years."

Feldstein was dead.

I got in his car.

I was finally rid of Feldstein.

It was too bad I had to lose him this way. **Q**

It's Argentina, Betty Flynn!

I'll tell you this one thing about Betty Flynn. Hey, we can't all be Albert Einsteins every blessed minute of the day, and aren't you glad of that? And you can say what you will, but she was a good mother to those babies, and it's a crying shame, a crying shame that it all had to turn out like it did. What I believe is that if she hadn't been caught dyeing those fried eggs that Easter, she might still be here; but who knows? What Hank said was that when he saw those green and those pink fried eggs on the children's breakfast plates, he just couldn't take it a second longer, and I'm not going to point any accusatory finger at poor old Hank. That man was long-suffering, and because he was long-suffering and a quiet thing into the bargain, folks just assumed he was having no truck with the whole business, but don't you believe a word of it. Why, one night I went over there, just a quick pop-in visit after supper, and that man was crying, let me tell you, crying his eyes clean out of his head, and there sat poor old Betty Flynn, bless her, rocking in the middle of the bed and singing "Bye, Bye, Blackbird," her theme song. *Pack up all my cares and woes . . .* I'm telling you, it just tears me to pieces every time I think about it. Rips me clean to shreds.

You know when I think it really started? With that earth obsession of hers. Remember how she was forever hauling a handful of dirt over here and saying how it was the only thing that truly mattered? Earth—owning your own earth—was what she said. Forever dropping down on her hands and knees like some dag-on dog sniffing soil. And there would be poor old Hank beet-red in the face, trying to yank her back up. "We're renters, ya'll know, and Betty wants her own place so bad she can taste it." But it was a lot more than that going on, if you ask me, and when she started ordering those five-hundred-pound sacks of soil to spread about the house, I knew big trouble was brewing up on the horizon. "It's my soil, because I paid for it," she'd say, as if spreading soil all over the kitchen floor was the most natural thing in the world to do. Kids loved it, of course. Precious little things didn't know any better and it had to have been fun making mud pies in the middle of your own bed. She even laid in a crop. Hand on the Bible, it's the truth. She once told me with the straightest face I do believe I have ever encountered in my entire life that she was growing corn in the living room. Help, is what I said. Help.

Now, telling a man that his wife may need some professional assistance in the mental department is not the easiest thing in this world to do, but I did it; sure enough did. Hank, dear boy, I said, I'm not much for doctors myself, but here I do believe there may be a demonstrable need. But the minute he would get up the courage to make an appointment, Betty Flynn would go as lucid as they come and she would cook and clean, stitch and sew with the best of them. "I declare, I do believe she's turned a corner," poor old Hank would say, and for a couple of weeks you'd think that whatever it was that had recently been askew had gone and righted itself. Wishful thinking, of course, but, hey, hope springs eternal.

But the real mistake everybody made, and it was a doozy, was in assuming that because Betty Flynn was sometimes a little vague that she was ergo stupid. Wrong, wrong, and wrong again. Even that irrepressible optimist Hank once sidled up and whispered in my ear that even though all the lights were on, he sometimes suspected there was no one at home, and I've heard some of the big mouths around here claim that she had always been two bricks short of a load. But Betty Flynn was a learned person, read all the time, and deep books, too. Just listen a minute and then you can judge for yourself what I'm saying.

One day we were all sitting out in the back yard having a glass of iced tea and Betty Flynn got that faraway look in her eyes and stopped talking. So I said, "A penny for your thoughts, Betty Flynn," and she said—are you ready for this?—she said, "Bolivia." I swear to God. "Bolivia," direct quote.

"Bolivia," I said. "Mercy. What you worrying about Bolivia for, Betty Flynn?"

"I'm not *worrying* about Bolivia," Betty Flynn said, "I'm just trying to remember what countries border it and I'm short one. There's Peru and Brazil and Paraguay and Chile, but there's one more and I can't picture it in my mind. Do you know? Anybody here know?"

Of course, everybody thought she'd packed up her common sense and run off with it to Pittsburgh, but later, after they'd all gone home, just for the fun of it I pulled out the atlas and sure enough there sat Bolivia with Brazil and Peru and Paraguay and Chile snuggling up close, and down at the tip was the beginning of Argentina. It was Argentina she was looking for, and so I went next door right then and there, and I said, "It's Argentina, Betty Flynn!" and she ran up and hugged my neck. Heck, I didn't even know where Bolivia precisely was, other than somewhere south of the border. But Betty Flynn sure did, and it impressed me no end, and it still does.

But then that toll-free 800-number business started up, which, as it turned out, went hand in hand with that earth obsession of hers and, for all I know, was probably linked in some obscure way to the dyeing of those fried eggs that last Easter. You see, there always was, shall we say, a method to Betty Flynn's madness. What Betty Flynn did was to compile a list of all the toll-free 800 telephone numbers she could lay her hands on, and then whenever she was thinking property, she'd up and dial one. How that got going was that she was watching some evangelist on TV and he started soliciting funds and said to call in your pledge to this toll-free 800 phone number. Betty Flynn did, and she pledged a thousand-dollar bill; that's what she said, "I'm pledging a thousand-dollar bill to aid in the Lord's work," and then she talked that operator's ear to paralysis. Remember now, they thought they had themselves a major donor dangling on the other end of that line, when in fact those poor Flynns didn't have a pot to pee in or a window to throw it out of. But as I was saying, Betty Flynn talked this operator's ear to paralysis about the importance of earth, owning your own earth, and said how she was looking to buy her own place. And then the operator said, catering of course to this high-flying donor, or so she thought, the operator said how it was mighty pretty down here at Virginia Beach, which was where she was talking from. That Virginia Beach had a nice, mild climate except for two months out of the year and was a perfectly wonderful place to raise kids, and for a while there it was Virginia Beach, here we come. But then Virginia Beach went the way of all of Betty Flynn's passions, because soon some operator at the Neiman-Marcus toll-free 800 number had her talking Dallas, and then it was San Francisco and New York City, you name it. What Hank said was that Betty Flynn would dial one of her toll-free 800 numbers and say, "Hey, how you doing today? This is Betty Flynn talking," and I guess they thought they ought to know her from somewhere or were maybe just killing time themselves, but before you could say scat, Betty Flynn knew all there was to know about Dallas or wherever, and was declaring to all and sundry that in a week or two they would be on that Greyhound and new-home bound. What finally tipped the scales, I think— although Hank didn't take her to the doctor until that Monday after that last Easter—was the afternoon Hank came trudging home from work, weary to the very marrow of his sad-and-sorry bones, and there sat Betty Flynn and those three babies, perched on packed suitcases on the front porch, ready, willing, and able at last to go. Not a stick of furniture remained in that house. Betty Flynn had called the auctioneer at the Bargain Barn and told him to come and get all her stuff and to sell it for what he could get, because, she said, the Flynns were leaving town. That was two weeks before that last Easter and for those two weeks all they had left to their name was a couple of throw-down bare mattresses to sleep on and paper plates and cups to feed themselves off of. And then she fried up those eggs that Easter morning and left them to soak in bowls of food coloring, and when Hank saw those green and those pink fried eggs on the children's breakfast plates, something snapped, I guess, and he said how Betty Flynn was going to have to go and see a mental doctor, because things had gotten out of hand, and that he didn't know anymore hardly what to expect from one minute to the next, and Betty Flynn said how she had grown pretty tired of all the uncertainty herself. She didn't put up a fight, not even a whimper, and I'll never forget the day they came and took sweet Betty Flynn away. I went out in the yard so I could wave her goodbye, and after about an hour, out came Betty Flynn accompanied by two attendants, I guess they were, walking as if dead lice were falling off of her and looking like death nibbling on a Nab. Drugged from here to kingdom come. I guess they were worried she might kick up a fuss, but there was certainly no straitjacket in evidence, or anything even vaguely resembling one. Just these two nice young men coaxing and teasing Betty Flynn out to the back seat of that long black car. Kids waved her goodbye and said to bring them home Baby Ruths to eat, as if she were just running to the 7-Eleven for a loaf of white sandwich bread. Well, I crossed over to her yard and gave her a big hug and said how she was to take good care of herself and that I would see her real soon, I was sure, and she just stared at me with this blank look on her face, as if she was trying to figure out who in tarnation I was. And then one of the attendants, trying to ease the tension, I guess, commented on what a nice day it was, what a cheerful sun we had shining down on us that day, and for a minute Betty Flynn seemed to snap back from wher-ever it was those drugs had taken her to, and she said, "A cheerful sun? Did you say a cheerful sun? Well, I'll have you know that's nothing but a pathetic fallacy," Betty Flynn said before she disappeared into the back seat of that long black car. One of the attendants looked at me for the longest kind of time, as if to say that what Betty Flynn had just said certainly did speak volumes, but I knew better. Later, after I had helped Hank to feed and to bathe those babies and to put them to bed, I looked up "pathetic fallacy" in the dictionary and, sure enough, just as I had suspected, Betty Flynn had been dead on center right. "Pathetic fallacy," in case you don't know, is the ascription of human traits or feelings to inanimate nature, like, say, a cruel sea or that attendant's cheerful sun, and once you've been made aware of it, as Betty Flynn made me aware the very day they took her away, you'd be surprised how often we all ascribe in any given day. Plenty, I'm here to tell you. And I'm here to tell you one more thing, and that's about ascribing, too. I'm never going to ascribe the word "ignorant" or the word "numskull" to my friend Betty Flynn, not in this life. Betty Flynn was not only crackerjack smart in the learned way, but ever since the day I went to see her in that home she's living in now, it's begun to slowly dawn on me that there may in fact be a rich vein of cunning in there somewhere.

You see, a couple of months ago the doctor told Hank in one of those sessions he's had to attend that Betty Flynn had been making remarkable progress, how she'd nearly picked their library clean of books, read everything she could lay her hands on, and how her recall of what she had read bespoke a keen intelligence, and that if things continued on the same course as they were on now, everybody felt certain she would be coming home real soon. And then, lo and behold, about two weeks after that, Betty Flynn suffered severe slippage in the predictable department, and when poor old Hank came over here to tell me, he looked nigh on to despair, every bit of which I can personally understand. I've been day-sitting those three babies of hers so that Hank can hold down a job, and I'm telling you, there are entire days around here when I can't tell my own head from a yawning hole in the ground.

Anyway, to cheer Hank up, I said I'd go to see her and tell her how the kids were doing and how we all loved and missed her and were praying for a quick and a complete recovery; and you could have knocked me over with a sparrow feather when I saw the home she's living in now. I'm talking Tara, honey; with beautiful lawns and a garden in the back for the residents to stroll in and a lake for them to sun themselves by. Well, they ushered me into this high-ceiling room with a fireplace in it that could have stood five broad-shouldered men, and in came Betty Flynn on the arm of an attendant, and it was step-pause, step-pause, like a bride, all the way across that big room. Well, I talked up a blue streak for the longest kind of time without much visible response from Betty Flynn, until I said how everybody missed her and loved her, and she finally mustered a small smile. And then I carried on about the mansion she was living in, what a beautiful place it was, like out of a storybook, and how I'd expected who-knows-what; cinder blocks and bars on the windows, I guess. And then I said that, even so, I knew how anxious she must be to get out, to get out and come on back home to her loved ones and how I was praying every day for that very result. And do you know what Betty Flynn then said to me? Hank don't even know this part. Betty Flynn said— are you ready for this?—she said, "It sure beats the pants off of Argentina, don't it? and home can just wait a while," is what Betty Flynn said. And when she did, my own heart leaped up into my very own throat, where it still this minute abides, because if Betty Flynn meant what I think she meant when she said what she said, then I can't help but spy myself on into perpetuity chasing after those rambunctious babies of hers, while Betty Flynn suns herself by that lake and reads more and more of those deep books and grows smarter and smarter all the while. But, hey, it goes against the grain of my very nature to impute negative aspirations to the benighted, and even

though there are times around here when I'd like to holler
Good Lord! right up to the skies, and would this minute if I
didn't have an inkling that it's probably another pathetic fallacy just laying in wait for me, even so, I'd still like to say it's
a crying shame, a real crying shame, that it all had to turn out
this crazy way it did. **Q**

Five Variations on a Duet for Fire and Staircase

A small band of flame is introduced at the foot of a simple wooden staircase, bounded at one edge by a plain banister and at the other by a white plaster wall. The stairs ascend to a small landing, from which they extend up in the opposite direction to the next floor. The fire consumes the first stair before advancing upward. The banister and the wall are spared until the fire reaches the midpoint of the lower flight, at which instant the foot of the banister and the baseboard of the wall begin to smolder, and by the time the fire has reached the landing, they have kindled and caught, and the smoke that rises from them acts as a pale gray scrim, behind which the flames, which are stretched upon the landing and which blaze there for several seconds before continuing their climb up the upper flight of stairs, can be seen flickering. Eventually, the lower stairs are reduced to embers and char, and the lowest ones begin to collapse. The banister is blackened in the wake of its fire, but several emaciated sections of it remain standing, and the wall continues to burn brightly, feeding a large reddish flame, which grows increasingly furious as it reaches the very top of the stairs. With a large crash, the wall collapses inward, bringing down what is left of the stairs and the banister, and causing chunks of glowing wood and sparks to shoot into the air.

A black-and-white photograph, which hangs on the wall on the way down from the landing, bursts into flame with neither warning nor apparent cause. Several quiet seconds pass while it scorches and then burns through the frame which holds it. The bottom post of the banister then also lights itself. The photograph falls to the floor, igniting the left side of the bottom stair; the flame on the post touches the right side, and it too ignites. The two fires burn in parallel and with remarkable speed up the landing, and while the flames they leave behind spread inward, they hover there in an uneven dance of heat, light, and architecture, which lasts beyond expectation, extending burn and time beyond what the materials would seem to allow, before falling and dying suddenly, leaving the upper flight of stairs untouched.

Here alone the staircase is a spiral of wrought iron, which winds up from the floor and disappears through the ceiling. Light falls upon it from a small round window set high in the wall behind it, casting swirled shadows onto the floor. The air is damp and chilly. Over a period of many years the iron oxidizes and the staircase drops slivers and flakes of rust to the floor at its own base.

Fist-sized balls of fire drop from the top stair, bouncing down from step to step like a child's toy. Some drop off the edge and expire on the floor below. Others track along the wall, rebounding from the back wall of the landing and hopping down the lower flight. Yet others become trapped against the banister's posts, and it is these which, feeding on the wood, set the stairs on fire. Patches of flame rise in several places and eventually conflate, growing in size as they diminish in number. The sound of crackling wood fills the air, but the fire gives off no smoke. From the upper floor, the sound of shouting drifts down, followed by muffled thumping and, as the conflagration suddenly swells, a faint, interrupted scream.

A sheet of flame covers the landing. It has been there for some time; it is possible that it has been burning for hours, even days, lying low upon the floor and undulating slightly, like water. Another hour passes before the fire splits; the right side rises and the left side begins to pour very slowly onto the top step of the lower stairs. When the two sections have made their way to their respective stairs, they stop and wait. The air

above the flames shimmers, so that the back wall of the landing, within which there is a large rectangular window, seems
possessed by a hot shiver. A small tongue of flame unwinds
from each autonomous fire and coils itself up a post of the
banister, stopping as it reaches that point of the rail which lies
directly above the burning stair. The fire seems to gird itself
before advancing, in one case up, in the other down, another
stair. No damage has been inflicted upon the stairs left behind.
Again the separate fires fall and rise in unison; again there are
moments of near-stillness. As the fire reaches the middle of
each flight, a tree, placed in the dusk outside the window,
abruptly explodes into flames. Burning leaves rise through the
air; blackened branches appear within the blaze that consumes
them. The fires upon the stairs do not move until the tree has
been destroyed, and then they resume their travels. Again the
stairs are unaffected by the flames that pass over them. As the
upper fire reaches the top stair, and the lower fire the bottom,
they settle and die. The staircase is unharmed. The window
has become opaque. **Q**

Hungry in America

So you start out hungry for a little cuntlet other than the little cuntlet you have waiting for you at home, and the next thing you know, you are driving around with what turns out to be a lot of cuntlet not your wife, a lot of woman who is a vision such as she is, who heats you even when you are alone, who says that she does hoodoo that you do not believe in, mostly do not want to believe in, are afraid of even if you mostly do not believe in, only hoodoo or not, believe or not, afraid or not, the next thing you know you are far from where you started out, far from the wife no longer waiting for you at home with the no-longer-yard-long hair: far from her and at that place in yourself where all that you have left is the knowing that nobody, that no little cuntlet, no lot of cuntlet, no hoodoo: not that you believe in hoodoo, and even if you did, that nothing other than just yourself is ever going to save you from yourself.

And so how I first met Sansaray—that is this whole lot of other woman's name, Sansaray—was while I was working the Pussy Galore and the DinoSores gig and standing down in front of the stage in front of those wall-high, wall-wide boom boxes: standing there in my grays, my Shadow Security gray pants, my Shadow Security gray shirt, with the Shadow Security patch on the sleeve, and looking at all that jail-quail-little-cuntlet with that rock-and-roll look, with that rock-and-roll-all-in-black-come-here-and-take-a-look look, with those little-black-underthings-worn-as-overthings, with those high black hump-pumps, with all that gold and silver sparkling on their necks, on their wrists, on their fingers: looking at all that kid-little cuntlet wearing what they wear, while me and the other men and women of Shadow Security were wearing what we wear: wearing our Shadow Security grays and standing between those kids and Pussy Galore's roadies with the tobacco chaws wadding their cheeks, with the ponytails hanging down the back of their *Pussy Galore and the DinoSores* T-shirts, with the belly rolls jiggling over their cowboy belt buckles as they swung claw-headed hammers down on the fingers of those shake-and-make-kid-little cuntlets that made it to the stage despite the men and women of Shadow Security, that made it to the stage and tried to get up and over to Pussy, only to come away with fingers pointing several ways at the same time. Many of those roadies, at least many of the roadies that I could see from where I was standing, stopped swinging their claw-headed hammers when seeing this one womanly lot of cuntlet, this one womanly lot of something that from where I was standing looked to me like she was a lot of anything she wanted to be and that later turned out to be Sansaray: that whole-lot-of-make-you-want-to-gobble-her-up kind of woman; that whole-lot-of-make-you-want-to-jack-rabbit-your-self-until-your-fillings-fall-out kind of woman; that kind of woman and more—in her black hump-pumps, in her black stockings with the rhinestones running up the seams, in her little black-and-white undersomething spotted and striped as if once belonging to some big make-believe animal, some big cat maybe crawling around in some jungle somewhere, and now and then crawling all over her, crawling up her, crawling up Sansaray's vajaguar so that you could see the groove of Sansaray's vajaguar; see that while seeing her big, her gigundo slurpies leaping all over, and her hair—man, what hair, hair black and curly and out there twice as far, blow-dried out there at least as twice as wild as any hair at that gig—her hair was almost as long as my wife's yard-long hair was, only black and blow-dried way out there; and there was also all that gold and silver sparkling on her neck, on her wrists, on her fingers, sparkling all over her, while she, while

Sansaray, sort of humped, sort of rode that blast of sound, until Sansaray, this whole-lot-of-hoodoo-or-so-she-later-said kind of woman, this table-grade kind of woman, this shtupperwear kind of woman with her vajaguar all out there and with her slurpies giddyapping all over her, reached up under her little black-and-white-spotted-and-striped undersomething worn as outersomething—but only going down so far, only just barely crawling over and up her vajaguar so far—reached up and yanked down her little V-sheath of panty undersomething, which she then stepped out of, which she then balled up in one bejeweled *uh, uh, uh* hand and sort of sissy-tossed toward Pussy Galore and the DinoSores, only for that lacy little V-sheath of a panty undersomething to then float, to then barely carry, to then unball and land *right . . . on . . . my . . . head,* with me looking out one of the leg holes at her, at Sansaray humping that sound with ten thousand million other screaming and singing Pussy Galore fans, not to mention the men and women of Shadow Security in their Shadow Security grays.

Meanwhile, the little wife still at home at the time with her still-then-yard-long hair was still trying despite herself, trying despite myself, trying with among other things those notes left on the kitchen table that started with "Dear Fuckface," and ended with "Love, your wife, who loves you despite myself, despite yourself, and who is at least trying, which is more than can be said for some of us"—and despite the despites, she did try—among other things, tried pulling me into the shower with the hot water sliding down us, with the shower drain clogged and the warm and the soapy and the scummy water rising up us, with my wife's yard-long wet hair all over us, with my mouth on my wife's mouth, with my hands on my wife's soaped-up slurpies, with my wife's hands on my soaped-up Elijajuan. And even with all that soap, even with all that trying, there was still no *"Oh, Jesus, oh"* from my wife, only more trying with the running-out hot water sliding down us, with the scummy water with the strings of dirt and with the clots of Elijajuan juice rising up us, with that look in my wife's wife eyes turning from *I'm trying, Chet,* to *What the fuck are we doing, Chet?* until that *we,* until that *us,* became that *I* . . . starting out, going out, ordering out for a side order of what I started telling you about.

So there I was, looking at Sansaray, the most lot of cuntlet looked at outside of a bone book, the most lot of anything I have looked at while looking out the leg hole of a little undersomething, while then taking Sansaray's little V-sheath of a panty undersomething off my head, while then handing that little undersomething back to her, to which she says, "Thank you", says, "Look at that big spook over there, look there, over there, coming over here with two beers in each hand"; says, "That big black giant of a son-of-a-bitch over there, that Dacey, that Dace, the motherfucker is driving me to hoodoo!"—while slipping around behind me, while holding on with both hands, while holding on to her little V-sheath of black panty undersomething while holding on to my arm, the arm with the Shadow Security patch on the gray sleeve; that arm that in high school almost had a muscle, only just that arm and only one muscle from scooping, from using just that arm to scoop ice cream after school; that soft but official arm there under Sansaray's bejeweled *uh, uh, uh* fingers, when this big black fucking spook with muscles all over, with big muscles in places I did not even have places to have muscles in, when this big black fucking spook of a man came over and says, "Oc-cifer," that is the way he said officer, says, "Occifer, whatever the probem," that is the way he said problem, says, "Occifer, whatever the problem here, I so big, so black, so giant of a spook son-of-a-bitch, that no problem, that no nothing, that no nobody wants to waste whatever little they got fucking with me"; and I say, "Yes, sir, only this woman, sir, this whole lot of heat-and-eat woman here, sir, is now in the custody of

Shadow Security for, for, for indecisive exposure in a public place with an occupancy of more than ten thousand people, sir, Dacey sir, if I may call you Dacey or Dace, sir, if I may call you sir, sir"—when the spook says, real soft, says, "Occifer, who's zooming who, okay?"—and this officer, me, I say nothing, not one word more, while putting on my best I'm-bending-over-and-cracking-a-smile smile, while giving him that smile with the lower lip up over the upper teeth, while backing up, while inching back, with Sansaray holding on to the back of my Shadow Security belt, with us— notice that *us*—with *us* inching back, tripping back over some of those screaming kids with their kid faces locked on Pussy Galore and the DinoSores, with *us* moving as quick-footed as *we* could move backward with Sansaray in her hump-pumps, with *me* looking at the giant spook, at that big black muscle of a man standing there looking at *us* tripping back through the crowd with *me* yelling, *"Shadow Security backing through!"*—until getting *through* and *around* and *backstage* to the band's way out of there, which was guarded with at least ten, maybe more, Shadow Security men and women, who let *us* back *by* and *through* and *down* the hall—and *out* the back way to the parking lot and *over* to the Shadow Security jeep, when Sansaray, still holding on to the back of my Shadow Security belt, says, "So how about a lift home"; says, "You look married"; says, "The hoodoo works in strange ways"; says, "Uh-oh"; says, "Look"; says, "Here comes the fucking spook"; says, "Drive, Mr. Shadow Security, drive"; so we drove.

So I drove—headlong.

Sansaray sometimes, one time, talked hoodoo in a way that was enough to make you wonder when she talked about causing snakes and spiders to spring up inside the body of somebody, although Sansaray said she only talked that kind of hoodoo and was not into that kind of hoodoo and that she was mostly, really, only, into uncrossing hoodoo, into doing hoodoo that was against hoodoo, and not really into snakes or spiders or anything like that, although Sansaray did say that she once did use a catfish that she had her brother Levon, catch and hold while she clipped off the three sharp spikes on the catfish's back, which she dried over a flame, which she crushed into powder, which she mixed with white pepper and then, or so she said, and then she wrote the name of the somebody, the name of Sansaray's second-semester math teacher. You see, Sansaray was in her second semester at Apex Tech at the time that I am telling you about—or so she said, and that she also said she would never do any hoodoo like this now, or like that now, although Sansaray said she did once do this kind of hoodoo to get a good lock on a neighbor's insides, so that the insides of this neighbor could not even come across with a Hershey squirt or anything for the rest of his fucking life. Then she wrote on a slip of paper the name of the some-body, this Mr. Amato, her second-semester math teacher at Apex Tech. She wrote his name three times across itself, then folded up the powdered catfish spikes and white pepper inside the paper and put the paper into the mouth of the catfish, then had her brother Levon, throw that fucking catfish back into the same part of the river that Levon had first got it out of, and within a week, or so Sansaray said to me, this Mr. Amato was teaching second-semester math fucking all-out-there naked from the waist down: naked with his little hairy woman bait hanging down, fucking naked like that, until Mr. Sullivan, Apex Tech chancellor, and Mr. Lemoyne, Apex Tech custo-dian, hustled Mr. Amato out of there; and that was the only time, that and her neighbor's locked insides, that Sansaray said she did that kind of hoodoo to anybody, and she was now only into uncrossing hoodoo, using roots to uncross hoodoo, using, she said, red-coon root, Solomon's red root, Come Back in One Piece root, Cast Off root, Hurry Up root, yaw root, Jinx Killer root, and some other roots I don't remember, because by then Sansaray was making me think only of my

Elijajuan root, even more than she had already been making me think of it.

Meanwhile, the little wife said what she said by leaving off the light, so that coming home late, coming home early, there was no light for me to see to put the key in the lock as quietly as possible, to close the door as quietly as possible, to tiptoe down the hall as quietly as possible, to heel off my Shadow Security boots, to tiptoe in my socks into the kitchen for a slug of milk straight out of the carton and down my chin and down my Shadow Security gray shirt to drip all over the goddamn kitchen floor, to read in the light of the open fridge the note left on the kitchen table that started with "Dear Numbnuts" and that ended with "You and your secret Shadow Security night assignments, come on, Chet, who is zooming who?" to put the milk carton away as quietly as possible, to tiptoe back down the hall as quietly as possible, to leave my Shadow Security grays there on the living-room rug as neat as possible, to lower my 157 pounds of no muscles whatsoever into bed so as not to disturb the person then sleeping the way she then slept, with her then-still-yard-long hair spread out on the pillow all around her, with her sleep-breathing the only sound other than the sound of the fucking fridge, with the set of her chin saying to me even in the dark, *Yes, Chet, you have pissed what we had away, Chet!*

When you find that little cuntlet that turns out to be a lot of cuntlet, the next thing you know you want to do, you want to go a little somewhere, like to Pizza My Heart on a slow Tuesday night to maybe order the Heart Stopper, which, by the way, is seven dollars and change a slice. So you order a slice of the Heart Stopper for her and a tall water for you, and you watch as the olives, as the hot sausage, as the shrooms ooze off onto her sweater-covered slurpies at their slurpies-at-ease, which you offer to clean off without using your hands, and to which she says, Yeah? So . . . then . . . you . . . figure you'll take her to Donut Master for doughnut holes, and watch as she scarfs down maybe half a dozen at three-and-change a dozen before heading back out to the Shadow Security jeep and to sitting there and telling her that *you have never felt like this before* and that you are going crazy to take her to some really special place, like probably to a Brew & Trough for the salad bar, only, hey, you are a right-to-the-point kind of guy, with the point suddenly being that you have got to slap a little Elijajuan on her right this very instant; then you say, in all *seriousness* now, with all *kidding aside* now, that what you really want is for her to throw a crotch-lock on your face until either her legs go numb and turn blue or until you drop dead from suffocation, whatever comes first, and that is exactly what the game plan was on that slow Tuesday night, with me wearing my best Shadow Security grays and driving the Shadow Security jeep, when there I suddenly am: out front of where Sansaray lives with her father, her mother, her grandmother, her four sisters, her brother Levon; out front looking in the bay window all dark except for the flicker of blue on the glass, and me honk-honking for Sansaray, for that whole-lot-of-hurt-me-good kind of woman, for that whole-lot-of-even-learn-ball-room-dancing-if-that-is-what-she-wanted kind of woman, for the whole-lot-of-spank-and-serve-fucking woman, and then that woman letting the screen door whack shut behind her while she clacks down the steps in her hump-pumps, then clicks down the walk with all that sparkle sparkling on her neck, on her wrists, on her *uh, uh, uh* fingers holding a little black kimono something up close to her as she clicks. So I reach over and snap open the door to give Sansaray a hand in, as it were, when she says, "You know, you still look married, only not as married as you looked before, Chet"; says, "We're staying right here, Chet"; says, "You can meet my father, my mother, my grandmother, my four sisters, my brother Levon, and some others that I want you to meet, Chet."

So we stay.

So I figure I saved big bucks by not going to Pizza My

Heart, by not going to Donut Master, by not going to Brew & Trough, and by going inside instead, but that leaves out, of course, totaling up certain costs, which you will see are to come later.

All the while, of course, there was less and less of the little woman still at home, less and less of the little wife—less, like no washing dishes, like no washing clothes, like no cooking food, like no talking words, like no leaving notes anymore, and like no fucking for the idea of home and hearth.

But I still come home and give her that "Honey, I'm home," and get back just the sound of running water until, after an hour of getting that sound, I go in and see her sitting there in the tub with a scissors in one hand and a clump of yard-long hair in the other hand, sitting there with the shower water shooting down at her, her face all twisted up in that weeping way they have, sitting there with clumps of yard-long hair floating all around her on the rising, scummy, way-too-cool-by-then water.

So there we were inside, in the living room all dark except for the big TV flickering *Fantasy Island* all over the walls, all over the ceiling, all over the faces and the hands of Sansaray's father, Sansaray's mother, her grandmother, her four sisters, her brother Levon, all watching *Fantasy Island*, with none of them even looking up to see me when Sansaray says, "This here is Chet of Shadow Security," with none of them even looking away from *Fantasy Island* when we go into Sansaray's room, with Sansaray clunking the door and snickering the dead bolt behind us, locking in what looks to me like a big wind had come through and blown all of Sansaray's shit all over the floor, all over the chair, all over the unmade bed, all over and hanging off the antenna of the little TV rolling *Fantasy Island* that we are now watching while sitting on Sansaray's bed, that little TV that Sansaray is watching while I help her take off that kimono sort of outersomething worn as

outersomething over her white-turned-blue-with-*Fantasy Island*
shoulders, over her strapless, shoulderless, cut-way-low-way-
down-to-there little pushup of a little undersomething worn as
undersomething, while I help her unzip the pushup little undersomething's zipper, letting loose her humongous slurpies,
while I help her slide down her little V-sheath of panty undersomething hiding her groove, her slice of hairy vajaguar, while
I help me unbutton, unzip, let drop my Shadow Security gray
pants, while I help slide down my Shadow Security gray skivvies, when Sansaray, without for one instant looking away from
Fantasy Island rolling blue over her white arms, rolling blue
over her white belly, rolling blue over her red slice of vajaguar,
says, "Wait, Chet"; says, *Fantasy Island* ain't over, Chet"; says,
"Dincha hear the door, Chet?" when I hear *thud, thud* on the
door and I hear her brother, Levon, shouting from the other
side of the door, shouting, "That big black giant of a spook is
out here with a whole lot of others, and that spook and those
others want to fucking talk to what's his name!" and Sansaray
says, "Tell that big black giant of a spook and all those others
that we are watching *Fantasy Island!*" and Levon shouts, "You
tell them yourself!" and Sansaray, without taking her eyes off
Fantasy Island, gets up off the unmade bed and goes over to the
little TV and turns up the sound and comes back over to the
bed, when there is a *thud, thud* on the door and a *deep, deep* voice
that says, "Occifer, I want to talk to you," and Sansaray, without looking away from *Fantasy Island,* says, "Talk to him,
Chet"; and the *deep, deep* voice on the other side of the door
says, "Occifer, there is no probem here that we cannot take
care of if we put our minds to it"; and Sansaray, without
looking away from *Fantasy Island,* says, "Put your mind to it,
Chet"; and the *deep, deep* voice on the other side of the door
says, "Sansaray, unlock the door"; and Sansaray gets up off the
bed without still looking away from *Fantasy Island* and goes
over to the door and grabs the dead bolt . . . when I shout,
"Wait!"

. . .

About my wife, you should know there was so much less of the less of the little woman no longer at home that there was only a note left on the kitchen table with nothing written on either side of that plain white notepaper other than "Dear Geekmonger."

As I was saying, there was Sansaray waiting when I shouted, *"Wait!"* and holding on to the dead bolt and watching *Fantasy Island* when that *deep, deep* voice on the other side of the door says, "Occifer, it is nearly time"; and no sooner does that *deep, deep* voice on the other side of the door say that than the theme music for *Fantasy Island* cranks up and Sansaray snickers back the dead bolt and comes back over to the bed, while the doorknob on the door slowly turns, while the door slowly opens, while the door slowly opens all the way for Dacey, for Dace, for that pumped-up, veined-up spook of a Dacey spook wearing *whites,* wearing Universal Security Service *whites,* make that Universal Security Service *white* gloves, Universal Security Service *white* pants, a Universal Security Service *white* shirt with the Universal Security Service patch on the sleeve; and from what I can see from standing there with my Shadow Security *gray* pants and my Shadow Security *gray* skivvies down around the tops of my Shadow Security boots, out there, out behind Dacey is Pussy Galore and the Dino-Sores, and out behind Pussy Galore and the DinoSores are Pussy Galore's roadies, and lined up and stretching out behind those roadies are those kid-little-cuntlets with their rock-and-roll look, and behind those kid-little-cuntlets are the men and women of Shadow Security, and from what I can see from just standing there, out behind those Shadow Security men and women is a pizza delivery man fucking all-out-there naked from the waist down, naked with his little hairy woman-bait standing out there like a shroom, and behind the pizza delivery man is a man standing there with his legs crossed, and lined up behind that man is Sansaray's father, Sansaray's mother,

her grandmother, her four sisters, her brother Levon, and behind her brother Levon, there is a man, no, make that a woman, a woman that is—my God—that woman is my wife—when Sansaray, spreading herself, spreading her vajaguar wide, says, "Now, lover, eat now!" **Q**

Certain Properties of Play

She would watch things around the house, would watch the doors, the windows, while they were down there, laughing. She would watch the moon, would go to the bay window to look out over the Sound, to see the lighthouse at the Point, were its lights still on. And she would straighten Bruno, her bear, slumped in his seat, so he could see them too, the lighthouse and the moon over the Sound. And she would look closely at his face, to see did he see them, and at her own face in the frame, to see was it the same as before.

Then she would put up the Palace of the Moon, the otto-man upside down, and would set out the things that were alive when no one was there. She would open the books to their best pictures and would rub her fingertips over the ridges of their spines to make them stand up. And would make a wall to surround the palace, to see that no stranger could come there, that no one could come out or get in without notice.

Then she would bring the Dresden Lady and the Bookend Man to dance on the Chinese rug, on the dusty-rose and the Chinese-blue flowers in the palace garden, and would watch them, the moonlight on them, they were so beautiful, so still.

Sometimes she would go to the piano to play music for them and would rub her fingers on the ivory keys to make them warm to the touch, and would feel the ebony keys, which were cooler, which were cool. She would make them make a chord and play that they did not want to, and would make them get out of breath, so beautiful. Sometimes she would make them get down low and sound like a storm, or animals growling, or noises like little raindrops. And then she would take out the sheet music that was there before she was born and would try to play it, the song.

She would count which keys for which fingers, for just the

right hand, for just the single notes, or the one on top, not the two together or the one with the many. She did not know the left hand, so she kept that one in her lap and tapped to keep time and tried to play the first notes of the song and would watch the hammers go up and down. She would try to sing it, "Serenade," but not to disturb them; *Serenade:* to entertain by singing or playing beneath a window to a lady, so that was right, was what the dictionary said, and of course she sang it under her breath.

This one time, she turned off the lights, so she could make it cool, so the moonlight could come in coolly by itself and shine itself onto the Chinese rug. And she brought the Dresden Lady and the Bookend Man to dance on the flowers, the roses and Chinese-blue flowers. And she presented to them the paperweight magic forest. And brought as a present to the Dresden Lady the silver-back mirror, so she could see how beautiful she was, how unchanged. And brought to the Bookend Man *The King of the Golden River* for his library, so he could read it whenever he wanted, so that he could go there whenever he wanted.

Then she saw on the mantel that the Marble Lady was watching, and that her skin looked real in the moonlight, only more pure, more cool. And she wished she could bring her down to the dance, to lie down and lean on her elbow among the blue-and-rose Chinese flowers.

So she climbed up on the ottoman to invite her and her twin behind her in the mirror, saying, *Are you lonesome?* And she touched her finger along the dent of the Marble Lady's spine, and down the ridge of her nose. The Marble Lady was looking away, leaning on one elbow, as she always did, and she did not have any clothes on top, because that is the way statues are, she thought, the way they are supposed to be. The Marble Lady's face in the mirror was a cool pure gaze.

Then she looked at her own face in the mirror and put it close to the Marble Lady's, and she watched their faces together, their pure cool gaze, and she thought to touch them, the little nipples. And she watched to see if the Marble Lady would change her expression. She touched them again with her fingertips; they were so cool, the little points, she had not expected it. It made her laugh under her breath, so she leaned over and kissed them, they were so cool.

Then she thought to climb down and to go upstairs and to touch him awake, her little brother. And when he opened his eyes, to put her finger across his mouth. And she asked him, did he have to go pee-pee? And when he shook his head, she whispered, Yes, you do, and took him there and unfastened him and asked him was he too sleepy to hold it and he nodded his head, so she held it for him, it was so warm, and she bent down and put her mouth on his. **Q**

James

Men walk on their tiptoes in my house, as if the floor might open up and swallow them. Most of the men are married. They set their coffee spoons on my counter without noise, the way you would if someone was sleeping in the next room. The men are nice to James; some play ball with him on the front lawn. James is slight and freckled like his father. Trusting.

There is an easy kind of orderliness to my house. My things are worn, from thrift shops, and I keep my copper fondue pot on a shelf next to a round-bellied clay soup pot with matching bowls. My fifties coffee table holds James's drawing things and my books. I hate the beige and silver-flecked lamp with its battered shade, but I forget about how bad it looks until I come home from a trip and see things the way a stranger would. But by the time I might get around to replacing the lampshade, I've forgotten about it again.

I have an antique grandfather rocker a married couple from San Luis Obispo gave me when I was nursing James. The rocker still has tiny milk spots between the slats, where I cannot reach with a cloth, but I like them there. The couple is divorced now, but the milk spots are still there. I would have thought the milk spots would biodegrade.

The men who visit escape their real lives and act like my things are partly theirs. They like to find my bar of almond soap hanging from its jade-colored string next to the bathtub and the Herbal Essence shampoo on the window ledge. They know where to find the utensils and the long stick matches to light the fire. We burn incense and we make love after James is in bed. Sometimes we fix a snack and talk until morning, and they leave when the light is still gray and depressing. Sometimes it rains and I just want to take a long shower and go back to bed, but I have to fix James's breakfast and get him off to school, then go to work. I work in a bookstore, Bach and Books on First.

Some of the men are famous and I go to their lectures and readings. In public we act as if we barely know each other. Before we go into the auditorium, we say we will go for coffee after, but we always come back to my house for Belgian waffles, which I make with wheat baking mix from the health-food store. We squeeze fresh lemon and sprinkle powdered sugar on top. After, we wash and dry the dishes and wipe the counters. Their wives no doubt have dishwashers. I would not use a dishwasher if I had one. People who use dishwashers are careless and use more of everything than they need. I use one mug a day for coffee and keep it beside the stove.

Although we never sleep well, I think men like my single bed pushed into a corner, as if I do not expect to sleep with anyone and what happens is a surprise. I had a water bed, but James's puppy chewed a hole through the vinyl mattress.

The men who visit wish they could live with me. I ask little of them and they assume this is the way it would be. I don't know why men are so stupid that way, but they are. They think their lives would be simple and they would know what they wanted if they lived with me. If it wasn't for their children, some say, they would leave their marriages. I am even-tempered, no premenstrual black moods like some women who act like trapped spiders. I hate the look women have in their eyes when they come into the bookstore and get completely frosted over nothing. Sometimes I am a little depressed and cry, but it is the soft kind of crying, and I save stronger emotions until I am alone. That's the way I want it.

I would not want to live with a single one of the men who visit, but I do not tell them this, because it would hurt their feelings. For some reason, I have always had a soft spot for men who seem like blown-up little boys to me. There was this kid Albert, in the third grade, who was Greek and who was completely uncoordinated. The boy fell a lot and skinned his elbows, and I watched him from my desk—I sat in the next row and a few seats behind—and I could not stop looking at those dirty, scabby elbows and wanting to cry.

I am very clean. I bathe twice a day and I wash my hair every morning. Nothing I wear gets worn more than once before it's washed. I even wash things that should go to the cleaner's, like light woolens. When I was a teenager, my mother and I lived in a flat above an inn, and drunks used to mistake our apartment for their room and try to open the door. I slept on a studio couch in the living room, and one time I woke to find a fat old man standing over me. The man did not hurt me. He said he was sorry and left, closing the door quietly, as if he wanted me to go back to sleep. Whenever my mother came home with men, I put a pillow over my head so I couldn't hear them grunting through the wall, and in the morning I washed the steps that led down to the front door with Lysol.

The men who visit think I want to be married. They don't know that I wake up screaming like my mother used to scream when I dream of getting married. I don't know what my mother dreamed about, but I dream of running through old, empty houses looking for a place to hide. When I get to the garage, the garage is filled with things a father would keep, like boats, skis, fishing poles, power tools—all hanging from the ceiling on large brass hooks in no particular order. Before the house dreams, I used to have the rice dreams.

It was in a place like heaven—all white and foggy—and I would be lying on the ground like a cloud, and I would be naked and completely covered with tiny pieces of something, and men would come and look at me.

I had not seen Stuart in four years, when he read his own poems at Bach and Books—he usually reads poems written by other people that he translates. I got to the bookstore late, I had seen a write-up in the *Weekly,* and I stood in the back next to a table where Stuart's books were being displayed—his last two books of poetry. There was a paper plate of little hexagon soup crackers on the table next to the books. From time to time, someone reached around me for a handful of crackers and chewed them next to my ear, so I could not hear what Stuart was saying.

From where I was standing, I could see that Stuart had turned into an old man with thin blond hair and a glob of white spit that kept collecting on his lower lip as he read. He had written his poems on wrinkled pieces of white or yellow note-book paper, and he looked at certain people in the audience, pushing his lines forward like shy children. He was big on the ironies of everyday life, and he asked us to forgive the people caught in situations that made them rude or self-centered.

After, Stuart came to me and we talked for a few minutes and I started to leave. Stuart followed me to the door of the bookstore and he asked for my phone number—I moved a lot. He said he would be in touch, which meant Stuart would call me within a half hour or so. He would come over and we would go to bed. It was a pattern from the years before. He never said things directly. Just as he took a long time leading up to sex with words. Some men got me wet with their hands. Stuart used words to lead up to sex and to take my attention away from his small penis. That's why he went down on me so much, I'm sure of it. Men don't really like going down on women, I don't think. How could they? Another thing: Stuart always made a big deal of coming. I never liked that in a man.

Soon after I got home, Stuart called and came over. We made love and fell asleep, and he stayed over, which he had never done before. In the morning, Stuart said he wanted to take James and me to the zoo. I didn't like the thought of it, getting wrapped up in a day with Stuart. It reminded me of a lesson my mother taught me when I was in grade school. I had put on my party dress hours before someone's birthday party, and I sat with butterflies in my stomach waiting for the party to start. My mother told me everything in life was over before you could snap your fingers, so there was no reason to have butterflies about anything.

At the zoo we bought Coke and hot dogs and spent more than an hour in front of the orangutans—James only liked the birds and the orangutans. I could hardly see them, I was so uneasy about spending day time with Stuart. I thought that Stuart's wife was probably out of town. I figured we would take separate cars and Stuart would head north from the zoo, but instead we drove up in Stuart's car, and Stuart said he wanted to drive back to San Jose along the coast so we could buy lobsters and cook them for dinner. I started to feel the way I feel in the rice dreams and I wanted to take a shower. I never take baths to get clean, I only take baths with men, so we can sip a glass of wine and be warm and comfortable. When men leave in the middle of the night, I always take a long shower to get clean.

Lately, I had been thinking about old women—the kind you see sitting alone in divey little coffee shops with their thick, wrinkled necks and limp hair. One time I saw a fat old woman sitting alone and the woman looked crazy, not as if she belonged in the café, and as if she would probably start talking to herself any minute. Then the woman's husband came with two cups of coffee and the woman looked respectable. It made me want to get married someday. Let's face it, I won't always be long and willowy, with a nice smile. You have to be realistic about your life.

One time Stuart and I made fresh lemonade, and I could tell by the way Stuart looked at me under the tree, with the light on and off through the leaves, and my white blouse held out in front and filled with dusty lemons, that Stuart loved me. I don't think it lasted very long, but no one ever looked at me like that. We went inside and used my grandmother's old orange-juice squeezer, and we made the most incredible lemonade, with just a little sugar, which was almost impossible not to gulp, even though I wanted to look sexy and not smear my lipstick. Stuart had this practiced look he could turn on with women, especially when he lectured at the university, a breathless "my God you are magnificent" sort of look when you would say something ordinary, and it wasn't that look, the way Stuart looked at me under the lemon tree. Stuart's face was out of control, as if he were going to cry, and I did not like it. I thought Stuart looked old and senile.

Anyway, we got the lobsters; they were smaller than what I had in mind, because we really bought only lobster tails, a bag of two dozen. Then we stopped at Marsh's produce and bought stuff for salad, several kinds of lettuce, some tomatoes and cucumbers. We bought French bread, and Stuart said he would make a great sauce from whatever I had in the refrigerator. The thing is, when you are a single parent, you keep only basic things, like ketchup and mustard, but I let it go.

When we got back to my house, I got out the Betty Crocker cookbook and Stuart took James down to the corner park. I wanted to go, but it seemed corny. As you know, lobsters don't take long to cook, so I got everything else ready and waited till Stuart and James came back from the park looking red-faced and sweaty. Men can focus on things when they are sweaty—it doesn't bother them the way it does women. Stuart pretended to like James, but I say it was an act. I'm not even sure Stuart liked his own kids. He was too wrapped up in himself, is what I say.

Stuart gave James a push toward the bathroom and told him to clean up, and he pushed him too hard and that pissed me off. I didn't say anything, but by the time we sat down to eat, my stomach was in this huge knot and starting to strangle me from the inside. Sometimes I get way too angry at things that do not make any sense.

Everybody ate their lobster tails with Stuart's ketchup, mustard, and horseradish sauce, and it wasn't actually that bad. James had seconds, the way he does when there's a man around, as if James is trying to show off what a little man he is. James loved it when whoever was there wanted to arm wrestle, but he got mad and cried if they didn't let him win. James always had to arm wrestle with me when there was a guy around, never when we were alone, and I always let James win. I didn't mind, and after, I grabbed James and I wrestled with him on the floor, so I could smell that sweaty little kid smell that would be gone in the snap of a finger.

I am very careful when it comes to money. Every paycheck I put fifty dollars in the bank for a rainy day, even when I need it for something else. I figure someday James and I will travel again, or James can use it for college. There's nothing on my mind for myself. I don't care that much about expensive things, like most women. Having a kid is enough for me, and some admirers to visit once in a while, to keep me feeling like a woman. Otherwise, you can start acting like a man. Sometimes I think about James growing up, and I wonder what I will do when he goes to do whatever he will do. I think I'll probably join the Peace Corps or get married. I can't think of much else. I've read all I want to read, so I don't care that much if my eyes go bad.

So anyway, we all finish eating our lobster and I clear the table and we do a bit of playing around on the living-room floor, James, Stuart, and me, and then it's getting late and I am expecting Stuart to make leaving noises. Instead, Stuart lights up a cigarette and turns on the TV. You can't imagine my surprise. Stuart knows I hate cigarette smoke and he usually smokes outside. But the main thing is the TV, and it's not even the news or some boring documentary. I'm thinking if only all the wet-pantied coeds could see him now. Next he'll be picking his nose and asking for a beer.

As I said, it was a Saturday, so there was no need for James to go to bed early, except that I could see James was exhausted from the zoo and from outdoing himself trying to impress Stuart. Since dinner, James's voice had gone up about an octave and he was ready to drop any minute. I'm thinking I should tell James to go to bed, but I'm embarrassed to, because James will raise a fuss in front of Stuart, but then I realize he'll embarrass me no matter what, because James is so tired he's out of control. James is pretty easygoing, except when there's a man around. So I tell James to go to bed, and we have a row, and I bear down and think to myself that Stuart has rows with his kids all the time, everyone does.

Stuart stays glued to the TV for a little while, and I honestly do not think Stuart hears us yelling a few feet away from his ear. Then he tunes us in, stands up, and he picks James up and starts tickling him. Stuart throws James over one shoulder and heads for James's bedroom. I can't believe it's happening, and I'm too surprised to be angry, while James cries and laughs all the way down the hall and I hear James being bounced on his bed. James's laughing turns to crying and he starts calling for me and I go for him, but stop in the doorway to James's room, because I see Stuart lying next to James with his worn-out gray tennis shoes sticking out from the bottom of James's covers. Stuart has got one of James's old story-books, one I read to him when James was seven or something, held up over both of their heads, and Stuart is reading from it so loud he drowns out James's yelling. I stand in the doorway watching and not knowing exactly what to do—neither of them knows I am there. So I turn around and walk back into the living room and I stare at the TV, listening to Stuart's voice growing softer as James stops yelling. Stuart reads for a while, and then there's no more yelling. Eventually Stuart stops reading, and I wait for Stuart to come to me. I'm not sure I want to make love two nights in a row. I never like the way I smell the night after someone makes love to me. I'm not even sure I want Stuart in my house, and I try to figure out what to do with myself when Stuart comes into the living room.

I sit on the couch waiting for Stuart to come; then I realize Stuart is not coming. I walk back to James's bedroom and I see Stuart and James sleeping side by side, red-faced, different genes, different faces, same bed. None of it makes sense and my stomach feels red hot inside. I say Stuart's name a few times; then I go to Stuart and shake Stuart's arm, but Stuart does not wake. I shake Stuart harder, but he still doesn't wake; in fact, he settles into a deeper sleep and he turns spoon-fashion next to James, Stuart's arm across James's hip. This is it. I hit the ceiling. I shake Stuart harder and nothing happens, and the next thing I know, I am pounding on Stuart's chest with my fists, just pounding away. I know I'm acting crazy, but I can't stop. I don't want James to wake and see this crazy thing going on, so I hold my breath and don't make any sound, except for the thudding sound on Stuart's chest. It is as if I want to get my fists inside Stuart's bones and flatten everything inside so there's nothing left.

Stuart wakes up and stares at me; then he grabs my hands and holds them out in front as if I am saying a prayer. It's all I can do not to scream at Stuart, but I don't. James opens his eyes for a few seconds and looks at us, Stuart holding on to my hands, then he closes them again.

Stuart rises from the bed, still holding on to my hands, and he pulls me into the living room. He tries to make me sit on the couch, still holding my hands, but I will not. So he sits and I stand for a while and eventually Stuart lets go of my hands, but I stay standing in front of him and staring at his chest, pounding on Stuart's chest with my eyes. We stay that way for a while without talking, and when Stuart is sure I won't do anything crazy, he stands and takes his jacket from one arm of the couch, and he leaves.

I take a long shower. But I can't sleep, so I fix a cup of coffee and sit at the kitchen table thinking about things—the zoo, Stuart and James. I can't believe it when the sky turns its depressing gray and I realize it's becoming morning. I have no idea what I've been thinking about that could have taken the entire night. I fix another cup of coffee, and when it's lighter James comes walking into the kitchen, rubbing his eyes. James's mouth is still sleepy, even though I tell him to rinse before breakfast, and he slides between the table and a chair—

James is so skinny he doesn't even have to pull the chair away from the table. He sits there waiting for something. Neither of us knows what he's waiting for till he wakes up completely, so we just sit there, waiting. Across the street an obese woman comes out of her house and begins raking the leaves from her front lawn. When the woman moves the rake, bands of flesh swing back and forth under her arms. I think to myself that I should be sure to marry before I look like that. The thing is, I know I'll never marry until I stop babysitting these married men.

I fix James's breakfast and take another shower, and Stuart calls and starts apologizing. Stuart says some things that do not make any sense, about me and James and Stuart's life; then Stuart starts talking about his son—he's around James's age. Stuart tells me some things about his son, about how his son catches a baseball in the park and throws it right into this pond, a new baseball and everything. Stuart tells me that every time he buys his kid a baseball, his kid ends up losing the ball or something. Every time. Then Stuart gets around to telling me his son has a bad heart. He says it as if it is supposed to explain the part about his falling asleep in James's bed, which still makes no sense to me. Stuart says his kid is going to die.

I just stand there wondering what I'm supposed to say. I have never met Stuart's kid, I have only seen pictures. I don't know anything about Stuart's life except from pictures, so how am I supposed to feel? I listen for a while, then I say I'm sorry. I say I'm very sorry and I ask questions about Stuart's kid and Stuart's life. I ask Stuart what he will do.

I stay on the line and I say I'm sorry again, and I listen while Stuart talks, but I'm wishing I had never let my life overlap with anyone else's. James turns on cartoons and things begin to sound normal again, so I say a few other things to Stuart and then we hang up.

I tell James I'm going to take a nap, and I go to my room, undress, and curl up in my bed. My thoughts come and go like clouds, so I know I'm falling asleep, and I try not to give in just to see what I'll think next. I think about Stuart and about Stuart's son, and try to imagine what I would do if I were Stuart. I think I would blame myself and think God was punishing me for not being faithful to my wife. I think I would say around two million Hail Mary's, and I'm not even Catholic. Then I would vow to sleep only with my wife, and not even do that much and only the normal man-on-top kind of sex.

But I tell myself I have enough to worry about. I can't go chasing after other people's problems. I wonder if Stuart will get a divorce. I imagine Stuart marrying me and carrying both of our kids, one over each shoulder, while they laugh and cry at the same time. I imagine Stuart taking our kids to the park and throwing around a baseball with them and then reading to them and then falling asleep in the same bed with them, and none of it makes any sense to me. **Q**

She had amazing powers
of persuasion

Walking the Tracks

Back from the Zionsville post office,
I see that things go forward by twos,
rail by rail, tie by gravel bed,
that what's been laid in by hand
settles and becomes truly local, part
of the strut and skew of place—
the way Jung said the body altered,
immigrant pelvis and skull grown new,
two generations into America.
And isn't this how we manage,
one thing or another, odd man out?
and isn't this why we hunger
for that conjoining third something,
molt, or future tense? As, walking,
I come to realize the tracks I see
are not lengths of alternate pattern
but shapes surrounded by abutting beds,
themselves, in turn, pitched rubble
flanked by the hard walls of the wood?
Down the line a train whistle
describes the edge sound cleaves from,
going out. I range along both sides
of the tracks, kicking up bent spikes,
the crimped casings of shotgun shells,
and am content to follow these rails
past wherever it is they lead me,
knowing they lead me home.

Fox Grapes

I missed them last year.
My father traveling north as ashes,
my mind was on something other
than the light. Curved in its sides,
I think I might only have glimpsed
the hard lip of the chalice coming
my way, dribbling holy communion.
I'd have dwelled in the withered stems.
This year, the summer still with me,
I found them growing wild up the hill—
purple, dusky, dime-diametered grapes
clustered on the climbing vine.
Not cloudy like frost grapes,
nor as small.
The air was heavy with their scent.
Bees swung drunkenly around me
and doves drank that cool slide of music,
the tonic of their song.
And though I had been brooding on
darkness, the seed's slow suction
further into the fruit, I was kindled,
flashed through with a new ferment.
And so make of those grapes a sacrament,
saying *autumn, father,*
unclouding the wine of the heart.

ROBERT GIBB

Williams in Autumn

October 4, 1961: the hawkweed
is bristling in the Jersey
meadows and the sidewalks of
East Rutherford are littered,
here and there, with hulls
from the horse-chestnut trees.
The end of summer is no poorer
for any of that. The cemetery's
snow-faced
doughboy stands
overlooking the pastures of his
republic. And at 9 Ridge Road
the old poet, beautiful and
bare of poetry, has finally
declined to rummage in the welter
of his years.
                    He is tired of
being a house whose rooms are
closing, stroke by stroke,
and now wants simply to sit
bathing in the light he thinks
is falling for the last time
into Yankee Stadium, flooding
the shapes of the players
and spilling into his room.
Whitey Ford's blurred body
flashes homeward and the game
begins deploying its economies
of force—*close,* Williams wrote,
*to the principles of physics
and lyric poetry.*

        Four innings
later, New York breaks on top,
one to nothing, Ford's string
of scoreless innings now a pure
abacus of twenty-one beads, and
Williams elated by the seeming
spontaneity of such control,
the pattern to its variations,
as in jazz or local speech.
In the bottom of the sixth,
the Yankees double their lead.
The game flows slowly through
the lineups one last time
as though it meant to go on
forever,
        the slant light falling
like something from Masaccio,
the *Expulsion,* perhaps, the way
it bathes the attendant figures
as they are about to move out
of Eden into the world of time—
NEW YORK 2—CINCINNATI 0—
of traffic and the evening news.

The Pumpkin Field

Now, at forty, I stand alongside the road
where often I have paused before, amazed
this year as always by the sight of so many
of them together, spread like a river
of rocks, or wheels of just-disked pasture—
dusty boulders glinting dully in the sun,
ruddy globes the color of goldenrod
and oak tongue. It won't be long now
before I'll see those small flames wagging
within the scooped-out skulls on window-
sills and porches, understanding why the Maya
worshipped gods, not in the coinages
of autumn, but in that one immortal metal,
sun-struck, untarnished by the passage of time.

Birthday

You can count them back across your fingers,
such certainties of waking, year by year,
in their sequence of weather and rooms—
and another thread of the shuttle across the loom.
You can add them together, or single them out.

The year I turned twenty-one, for instance,
it was Syracuse and Russian, the Cyrillic alphabet
spread before me like a wrinkled swatch of silk.
The one after that was in Texas,
and by the following year's I was married.

I counted autumns down through the cornfields,
eleven moons through the tubers of spring . . .

Now, once more, I am trying to explain about
the grief of things in August, that weight
sunk down inside its skins, how the energy empties
from the roots and rot lavishes the ripeness,
how long a diminishing the end obtains.

And how birth's the beginning of longing,
no matter which direction we face.

On the Removal of Whitman's Brain

It must have shimmered, sloped like an island,
something of Paumanok's tides caught in crevices
where it heard the call of that widowed Alabama
bird,
    its folds like the negligent field of his woolen
comforter, a gray mass shifting toward the scent of
   lilacs,
quivering in the technician's hand,

                as if his trepanned ghost
held a butterfly to light that shone from his eyes,
through his spirit's vague walk, his ego's envelope
torn from this dismal flab,
                      this hump of metric custard
measured by trembling fingers,

                as if Mickle Street, noisy
                 Camden,
industrial fumes drifting across the river
into an upstairs window, were memories too heavy
for the analytic balance,
                  all those hours he lay
on the floor, unable to move, his untidy papers,
reproachful letters, a garrulous trail toward the
   doorway
he wished he could stand in, waving sadly like Lincoln,

                  eyelids working rapidly
until smog cleared from the unaccustomed
couplet of his lips, words running free,

            like that woman watching twenty-eight
           men
bathing in the river, her astral body splashing beside
    them,
slight hands the measure of bulging white bellies, thrill
    of
touch,

        alas, the bunched ganglia, the glowing pinpoint
of his hearing, the lingua franca of each groove and
    gnarl,
    alas, alas,
           it must have rolled when it hit the floor,
surging against gravity, heaving westward,
it must have formed like a flower about its clipped
    medulla,
gone flat as a nebula seen edge-on,
                suddenly swelling,
attracting dust motes, round knobs of drawers pulled
    open,
water sloshing upward in beakers, everything
    unfastened
flying toward it,

        tumbling the way planets fall into a dead sun.

Thinking of Gustav Klimt, with Molly on My Lap

It is her favored-cat's position: kneading me
with her clawless pads, purring, her green reptilian eyes
studying white words on the PC screen, waiting for her
     name
to appear. Her pupils dilate. Rain lashes against the
     window.

A whir
of gold in my mind; a woman emerging, as from a
     gold-leaf
quilt, extruded, bare-breasted, a metallic tapestry
what the world becomes behind her, the bursting of
     body cells
into their elements: auric arrangements of eyes, silvery
traces of an artisan's fingers,
                              Molly pushing her paws
into my velour shirt, imprinting it, now licking the
     white
border of her natural white ruff, now crossing her white
paws, suddenly quiescent,
                              and Klimt's *The Kiss* begins
to glow in a crowded room, where men and women
     jostle
politely, perfume mingled with nicotine, eyes flashing,
where man and woman fuse into a column of
     weightless
colors, the woman's uplifted face leaning into her left
shoulder, his hands stroking her cheek, her temple,
tendrils coiled around her ankles, for she is on her
     knees,

where he is simply phallic, emerging from a ground
of broken glass,
          and Molly begins kneading again, the rain
at forty-five degrees against the window, kitchen vent
clanking in the wind,

     and it's Klimt's *Salome* holding
John the Baptist's head, her fingers supple as young
bone, his closed eyes like a man's grown tired of
    reading,
no blood here, no redness, just her brownish nipples,
broken spirals, caught currents of air, her profile
ecstatic,
        and Molly getting bored, looking at these words,
my hands clicking the space bar at the keyboard,
Molly turning in my lap, her paws on my chest, moving
rhythmically toward my throat, while she pushes into
    velour,
     into the dry silence of a darkening room.

Escape

My family's history
    wasn't interesting
        enough to bury.
We allowed
    our wounded to fall
        without ceremony,
and now they
        can't be rescued.

Aches accumulate
        like pennies
        in a jug
    until we're too full
        to move,
but pain roots us
        finally
    to an empty room,
        not a battlefield.

I lay down
        my weapons
    because a child
    I love
        dreams
        my war.

The Killer

The Watchmen clock
    in the store window
    approaches midnight,
but Haight Street
        is migraine-bright
    and ankle-deep in disease
as he walks toward
    the bus.

He flashes his transfer
    like a badge
        when he boards,
then uses its cryptic symbol
      to ward off anyone
    nearing his seat.

Graffiti blur
      into animated cartoons
    as he stares through
    a toxic haze
    of germ-fogged mutants
      with carcinogenic hair.

Light coils like a snake and retreats,
    incubating death in its wake.

He rides home
    to burn his clothes
    and pray
      for anonymity.

For Janine at Six Months

You are royalty,
    Your Shortness,
and all within the kingdom
                  of your voice
      are subjects.

I envy your quick amnesia.
Your freedom from tomorrow
        is a brief immortality
    Later,
      when your toothless squeals
        calcify into language
      and your memory
          judges each moment,
      you will hate pauses
        worse than shitty diapers,
    worse even
      than having your nose wiped.

Now your belly button
              has nearly sunk.
    Your weathervane mouth
        contorts storm warnings
    into a crooked grin,
      fine-tuning
        your song.

Excuse

I think the trigger
            in my head
        is a vestigial Irish gene
        that shakes me
                with adrenaline
            during its ancestral wars.

The fault
        crosses both hemispheres
            too deep for scrutiny
                    or sutures.

Like a church bell
unable to shape time,
                I ring
            the hour
                at hand.

Dead Reckoning

These days
   something blocks the sun.

Instead of fate,
    only consequences
  are visible
    among the shadows
         ahead,
and when I turn off
  the lights at night,
    the last image,
  frozen in the phosphor
     of the TV,
is never history.

I've climbed too long
   on my own
        wreckage
  to ever escape
    uncertainty.

This moment and I
  are strangers
    spliced together;

our secrets,
   like a stolen masterpiece,
  are too recognizable
    to share.

Blue

On a round-shouldered day when the sun
sticks at 3 P.M. and grease drips
from the oil pan under the sky,
when a child's wail
slits the street's tight skin
and the hopes of summer are frying
on sidewalks—
a chicory-blue truck passes on slippers.

A blue truck slides down the slack vein
of the afternoon,
close-packed pigment boxed for shipment
to lakes and mountains sulphurous,
larded, waiting for blue . . . Ahhh!

In Lima, one gut-weary peasant
touched the Virgin's robe, and now
her rough hands brim with lapis light
no matter what she holds.

My Mother's Fears, Seen from an Airplane

Not those volcanic needle peaks casting knife-
blade shadows that slice down into the earth
and vanish.
No.
Those khaki hills standing in pools
of darkness that spread slowly across the plain
where we both live.

And Electra?

And Electra?
How was it for her?

I can tell you how it was for her.

I can tell you that from her father she learned
how to speak with few words
fix faucets
watch the sky
feel the warning signals of her mother's storms.

I can tell you how she felt
the night she skipped down the street to kiss
her father coming home from work:
she was happy to be on the right side.

I can tell you how it was for her later
when her father said he was going to be there
the day they found the cure.
When he cried because he could no longer push
    the lawn mower.
When hard small oblong pellets rolled down
inside his trouser legs and along the ground.
When his face turned to the face
of a man who is saying goodbye and cannot find
    the door.

Incandescence

Just as you ring the doorbell,
I finish reading Barth's account of what happened
when pirates flowed across the whoreship *Cyprian*
and took their booty in every part of the ship,
including the rigging, where one of the women
    clung
until her pursuer came up and upon and into her
    from behind,
while a crew member watching from the deck below
clapped his hands and laughed

just as you ring the doorbell

your coat already unbuttoned

already thrown on a chair
already joined by your trousers and briefs

your legs already bearing us to the bed, where
I smooth the fine straight reddish hairs that lie
in quiet rows across your belly
and remember other pirates I have read about

such as

victorious armies settling accounts.
In landlocked cities where there were no riggings,
they pursued their booty to the tops of towers.
In riverside cities, they nailed the women
naked and alive to doors and sent them floating
down to the sea. Flowed around and through

the ruins, calling "Woman! Woman!" Here the
    ships
were the churches, where the bells rang wildly
all night long. By morning, when the men of the
    cities
came with wheelbarrows to cart their women away,
the thick soft ropes of the bells were swaying
    slowly.

From these scenes I turn away
turn back turn away
wantingnotwanting to watch.
Turn away and stroke you there
and think about

my unit of female partisans, pouring out from the
    forest,
falling upon you hurling you down spread-eagling
    you
pegging you to the ground
while I
fumbling in your trousers
draw it out into the chilly air.
Perhaps I enter it with the long nicked blade
of my knife. Then we melt back into the forest,
leaving you to water this one small piece of earth
with your blood. Or perhaps we take turns
lowering ourselves upon you, cursing
when you do not rise to meet us. Until,
tiring of you, I order you taken
to the woods and shot.

The Underside of the World

Don't die in China,
my son says,
leaning against me at the front door
as he leaves for school,
his Bison baseball cap askew.
He's off to the corner yellow bus,
I to the underside of the world—
Beijing, Nanjing—
who knows where?
My suitcases, two sentinels,
guard the sacred doorway.
Please don't go, he mumbles.
But I must. Plans set in motion
lifetimes ago lead me inexorably
to the Lung of the Cow Gorge,
the Dipping Dragon Cavern,
the Fragrant Stream of the Forgotten Princess.
Goodbye. Goodbye. The child
grabs his sack of books,
makes a dash for it.

In a Distant Country

Navigating the Three Gorges of the Yangtze
takes all his concentration
so Captain Chao Wen does not smile for three
   days.
My gray-faced guide gives me names
for everything: This is the sea-slug soup, this
is the Peak of the Wounded Stork, this
is the Dark Cave of the Unlucky Brother.
This is the man you will not see again.
Look, here is the rock named Coming Toward Me.
It may be true, he says, it whines
and whistles, beckoning.
The Captain pays it no mind.
The mind is a rock named
Coming Toward Me.
It lodges here, in my swift currents.
If I should reach to grip its jagged edges,
it will slit my fingers,
spill my blood into the humming river.

Mohawk Working High Steel

If you were to ask him
how he knows the steps up there,
how he can stand to look down through clouds
and not feel the concrete call his bones
or hear a light static in his skin,
he would say only,
Where you are going
is where you have been.

This may help explain.
Picture a mind
in which history is biography.
Place it in an Iroquoian skull.
Knowing what it would know,
could it even imagine
two such falls in a single life?

Now

I hate them
for what
they have
which is
what I need
which is
what they're keeping
far away
from me
under layers
of
cotton
talk
and skin
so they can act
like they don't
even have
what I want
but they have
it
I know
I came out from
one
and I want
one
to open up
for me
again
now

View from the Top

I wore something
black to show you
my breasts
darkest dark
against lightest skin
to make you
want what
once you could have
loved taking
too long to make
your mind
about my shape
it married
had children
created history.

She tried to commit suicide in her friends house

BROTHER TRUTH this is me YOUR DISTANT SISTER with further words of praise. This is now the 9th letter I have written for your sake. My momma I told you of last time and the many times before goes on cursing you and calls me the most foolish-hearted sorry thing yet born for these letters to you. But it is the truth what you say. She dont know a thing before God nor man. Try like I do to tell her she dont. She goes on and clothes her self in costly attire to Gods displeasure and blasphemes. Claiming shes a God forsaken one and so are we all. But I hold my hands before my ears at such times and listen to Gods words you send to me about her and not to her. Yes she is best named MOTHER LIE for such acts and words.

Yes I do daily as you say that she may be transformed and not bring Gods wrath on her self. I have the imprint you sent me of your healing hand and I lay it on her in her sleep nightly that she may thereby be healed. Pray God our efforts on her behalf bear fruit in time.

It lifted my heart God knows how to have you mention me among the far away friends of the ministry last night. Your message leads me to write with this new offering such as it is BROTHER TRUTH and to claim your words for me. I know in time unknown to us here on earth supernatural blessings shall be witnessed by us all and we shall all reap the harvest of righteousness in Heaven.

And heres my tea spoon of salt wrapped in tin foil for you. Pass over it with your Sanctifying 7 Holy Keys for me right now as promised please. Break the bond of them that would speak our names backwards and burn black candles against us BROTHER TRUTH.

I pledge none shall make prey of me with their wrongful ways. Them that would shall not find their way into this house to make me their captive. They shall be made captive their own selves by their own devices in Gods time I know.

Yes I have often read the letters of Paul to Timothy. Yes I know the truth of 1 Timothy 4 and 2 Timothy 3 and 4 Praise God. I stand in knowledge with 2 Peter 2 and the Psalms of Deliverance.

I get your station clear on my radio at night but cant pick you up when it is daylight for other stations coming in to banish your Healing Ministries and Redeeming Words. The voices of others try and overcome you but never can for long. The Voice of Righteousness and the Words of TRUTH shall be heard over them that would deceive and lead astray.

I praise God your radio ministries reach me here despite the miles and them that would keep your message silent so none might hear and reach glory some day.

May God for ever and always keep tame the tongue full of poison for our sakes BROTHER TRUTH that the Way of TRUTH shall not go on being spoke evil of.

I continue to suffer these wandering pains in my body here below as you know and find it hard to sleep of a night. Your words spoke to me and my suffering last night though and ministered like the first night of bodily torment I suffered through till I heard. The Voice of God is sweet indeed to hear. More sweet and soothing than milk or honey and a joy to be heard by ear and heart of hearts alike. O to be baptized in the Healing Spirit for ever and ever night and day by your ministering voice BROTHER TRUTH.

I shall strive to keep my hands on my radio like you say and my eye on the dial. I shall hold my mind without wavering on Heaven and the inheritance awaiting me there as I hear you BROTHER TRUTH. Your voice may get distant with my hands away but it comes back to me in time. I fail to hear the crackle and static of your Godly voice coming over the air from so far as I listen and keep my hands nearby. Your Godly voice rings true and clear to me here despite the miles and them like MOTHER LIE that would harden their hearts to your words and all good news. You know it is not for me or her either one to speak against you and your so Godly ways.

You minister to me in my troubled and burdened life but I know. We all have our trials to endure in our earthly times. I know it is the truth what you say and what you send me in Gods words and material goods shall comfort Praise God. Praise God your words carry like they do over the contrary air between me and you BROTHER TRUTH. We are close in spirit though not in bodily form.

Yes I continue my watch on Gods Money Seeds you sent me last time for the supernatural growth of my earthly finances. Yes I wash my body from crown of head to toes of feet morning and night in my Money Soap. I shall get that filth and stink of thinking and doing no good off me if its the last thing I do so help me.

I can not call you on your Spirit Line any more for my Special Healing and Anointing Message and Spectacular Three Fold Glory and Blast of Everlasting Breath of God recording. MOTHER LIE had the telephone here unhooked day before yesterday.

Yes my strife and various trials are like waves driven by the wind of Satans rank breath from foul Satans lips in the Pits of Hell. Yes it is TRUTH. We are none of us beyond the bodily pains and miseries of the everlasting flaming fires of Satans deceitful ways.

This last 6 dollars I send as my Radio Broadcast Offering and Spiritual Gift to you BROTHER TRUTH. Now please send me the Special Prepared Money Bag you are called upon by God to make available to me right now. This is very important to me and my life of misery and everlasting woe. Please send me my Special Prepared Money Bag to settle me and relieve me of my hardships right now. I know it is the TRUTH what you say. It may be but a life of unbound misery for some here below. But we are not beings born to endure for ever the multiple curses Satan sends to curse us in our lives. Nobody but MOTHER LIE tells me any different from what I get on your radio station at night. I shall go on listening to your sound doctrine and shall not turn my itching ears away from TRUTH.

My street me and MOTHER LIE live on is same as it always was so please send me my Money Bag right here. The 18 dollars for my Unfading Crowns of Glory and True Master Keys to Lifes Material Goods and Earthly Riches is going to keep me seeking till I get it to you some day.

Yes I shall go on seeking to sow bountifully so as to reap the same in time. I shall give with my right hand in secret that my left hand may not see.

I kept aside 4 dollars clear and free to send to you but it didnt last me like it never does for long. MOTHER LIE found the 4 dollars in my dresser drawer and took it for her own unGodly purposes. Yes the TRUTH is my left hand is MOTHER LIE.

Yes I do trust you when you say my Gifts and Spiritual Offerings shall bring my riches and rewards forthcoming. Yes theres hardships to endure till that time. It is all in Almighty Gods good time I know. God knows the pains I suffer in my spiritual heart and He knows what it is I need before my prayers ever get prayed before Him. Miraculous God!

The pains I suffer daily get almost too much to bear some times as you know. Yes I have read in Job and certain Psalms and see what you said last night rings true. Even the blameless and upright suffer while the sinning wicked prosper.

Yes I see what your Eye of Eyes tells you of me is true and straight from God. I too seek to become an instrument of Almighty Gods good wrath.

I know it is the truth in Gods name what God told you to tell over my radio last night as every night. Yes BROTHER TRUTH. Yes, yes. Praise and Glorify God! I know the strife we suffer here below comes on by evil works of others and not by the good fruits of Gods vine and our righteous living before Him.

BROTHER TRUTH my street me and MOTHER LIE live on is same as always so send me my Special Prepared Money Bag for supernatural financial growth right now please. Unleash me for all good things happening right now and everlasting. If you can see your way clear to send me just a sample from that Money Bag you told about last night right now. It would be a blessing and weapon against them here that would keep making me out to be something I am not behind my back. Them that would renew the bond. I shall pray their hundred fold schemes to hurt me get paid back supernaturally in time Praise God. I patiently await the striking of Gods Mighty Sword of Judgment and foul Satans comeuppance on that great and fearful day as do we all Amen.

I just ask that you help me unbind these chains you have seen with your Eye of Eyes on my soul and let me soar to my due rewards in Gods time. Cancel that bond BROTHER TRUTH. Break these chains that bind YOUR DISTANT SISTER to hardship. I know theres some still yet like me and you to fight Gods good fight unending and not give heed to the doctrines of devilish men.

You know I hold steadfast and stable to the end my BROTHER TRUTH. To keep watch for Gods Money Seeds to sprout and flower in His time and that Money Soap to wash my earthly failings away. To go on listening to the Words of TRUTH. To keep devoted as always to what you are called upon to tell me and not to listen to the voices of false prophets coming to me from out of the darkness all around.

I trust you shall for ever and always be known by your works BROTHER TRUTH. May God give you His just rewards in His time too, so help me. Praise Almighty God!

> YOUR DISTANT SISTER
> *Enrolled In Heaven Beside You*
> *As Always Amen* **Q**

Michele, who used to be Fonseca, who used to be Trina, who used to be Babs, had been one of the lucky few to have pioneered the dragging of dead dogs by leash along the Avenue, but she had been quick enough to drop that when she noticed many others along the Avenue pulling the carcass of some recently deceased pedigreed. She talked with her friend Basil, who used to be Colin, and he suggested rat on a leash.

"It's certainly a lot easier than pulling a dead dog," he said.

"Who else is doing it?"

Basil wasn't sure, but then Michele knew that Basil wasn't sure of anything. It was this fog of his being that she found so appealing.

Michele shuddered when she remembered how close she had come to taking part in chicken on a chain, a thing started by someone who had no sense of what things are about. He was a loner, one of those who try to start things that mock things.

Michele visited the man who sold rats. He pointed out a large, sleek, brownish creature who was highly agitated when they approached his cage.

"His fur shines," the man said, "and not just during the day."

"Does he like to go for walks?"

"He likes lots of things, especially food."

"Would you have something I could put around his neck?"

"I wouldn't put anything around his neck."

Michele bought him and took him home. When she unwrapped the cage, his teeth were clamped around the chain link and his long, snakelike tail woven through the mesh. He hissed at her, jumped up and down as if the floor was burning. He was a very large rat. She placed him on the floor and found her old Lhasa apso's leash. She was anxious to begin. Currently, the Avenue was full of people waving dead cod.

Michele reached down to grab the rat by the back and slip the leash over his neck, but before she could grab him, he neatly removed the tip of her index finger. While he was chewing, she slipped the leash over his head and pulled tight the choke chain. Still bleeding, she hauled the squealing beast down the stairs and onto the Avenue.

The Avenue was choked with cod wavers, but the huge rodent soon cleared a path, and then the block. Alone on the Avenue, Michele was terrified, and dragged the squealing rodent back to her apartment. She called Basil.

"I need to see you. Right away."

He was a tall, strong-looking man with a strong jaw and strong teeth and weak-looking eyes and hair.

"I need to know if you saw anyone else doing this," she asked.

"Of course I did."

"I need the truth."

"I'm sure I did."

His lack of certainty she suddenly found very reassuring.

"I'll need some help," she said.

He looked at her blankly. A relaxing shudder went through her.

"Do me," she said.

"But hardly anyone is doing it anymore."

"Do it."

Michele bought a heavy pair of leather welding gloves to lift the snarling rat from the cage. She wore heavy boots, and stepping on the rat's paw to distract his teeth, she snapped the leash to the collar around his neck.

There were few dead-cod wavers on the Avenue. As soon as they saw Michele and the snarling rat, they fled. She had the Avenue to herself. Terror and fear mingled with an odd sort of water excitement, as if oceans were rushing from her body. She screamed, ran back to her apartment.

Basil was still there.

"I'm all alone out there," she said.

Basil said nothing, simply staring at her with that marvelous uncertainty.

She went out again, feeling depressed. She was unable to loosen a kind of clamp that fastened itself around her, as if it wanted to separate her into sections and let each fend for itself. The rat was skitterish. Michele had to kick it. She recognized in herself a sort of grim determination to be here, to be doing this. She thought that she, the rat, and the leash were as real as the molecules that make up jellyfish.

A cod-waving lady, furious at having been preempted, her hair stiffened, ran down the Avenue yelling, "Pigeons in my hair, pigeons in my hair!" As she ran by Michele, she glared at her, daring her "being" to match what was perched on her head. The following day, the lady became more desperate, baring her breasts, one of which was larger than two of Michele's. But with each failure the cod-waving lady seemed to shrink, curl over, as if her entire being was a question mark. Even her much admired breasts were smaller, less intimidating. Michele noticed her huddled over, twitching her body in small spasms of congeniality as she tried to engage each passerby in a small pile of sticks, much like a child who has made a discovery adults have long been aware of. Michele felt she was watching the disintegration of the verb "to be."

The next day, it was a young boy with a huge rat on the end of a rope. The boy's rat lunged forward, catching him off balance, dragging him toward Michele. She braced herself, boots slanted against the pavement, but her rat dragged her forward, consumed with hatred. The meeting of the rats was almost cordial, but it was over too quickly to tell how cordial it might have been.

The next day there were two other rats on a leash; one a huge, white-haired creature whose hair tips were yellowed and the second a copy of her rat, pulled by a woman who looked distressingly like herself.

She was lying in bed, entwined in Basil.

"I have to know," she asked him. "Is it me?"

"I suppose so."

"No supposes."

"I would say so."

Days went by when she was the only rat on the Avenue. She and Basil were sitting on the bed. "Do me," she said. "People don't do this anymore," he said. She took off his pants. She made him lie down. "I think it's the rat," he said.

She sniffed the air before she took the rat down to the Avenue. She had a strong urge to squat and piss. She was the only rat on a leash. Her "being" seemed fatter than she had ever remembered it. She was not afraid. Terror was the province of the thin. A man approached, selling machine oil.

"Oil for what?" Michele asked.

"For the wheels," he said.

She ran back to her apartment. Basil had caught his finger on an illustration in the *Guinness Book of World Records*. She bit him.

Most of her clothes were off when Basil left the apartment. She was too tired to put them on. The rat kept running around in circles, tethered to the chain on her wrist. He didn't seem to want to bite her. She let him sniff her.

The next morning the Avenue was crowded. People were excited, beaming, humming. Michele noticed fifteen, twenty rats on a leash. It took her breath away. The woman with large breasts was riding a huge stuffed rat the size of a pony. She hissed at Michele, "Rats in the hair, rats in the hair." Michele looked around and saw that the rats were stuffed, that the squeaks she heard were made by tiny wheels that had been sewn into the rat legs.

She had tiny wheels sewn into the legs of her rat.

She felt free, stuffed with unbeing. **Q**

—You said you were cruel to him. When were you cruel?

I was cruel at the beginning of my life and will be cruel at the end. Once, I told him I wished he was dead. And once, he reached out to touch my hair, he wanted to comb it, but I ran away.

—Now he's an old man and you regret such indiscretions. He writes you letters.

Yes, yes, letters about "The State of the Soviet Union," "The Problem of Quarks," "Proper Uses of the Nine-Iron." Pages and pages. Descriptions of arguments he wishes we'd have, engineering feats, revisions in the third law of thermodynamics.

—Your father's a scientist.

Of the worst kind. Expert amateur in every field, a man with reasons and ideas, inordinate confidence, a terrifying certainty regarding the order of things.

—And your mother?

Generally modest and unassuming, a hater of snobbery and peevishness in all its forms, a bridge player, brown-haired, barely five-foot-two, a streak of feistiness well hidden below the surface. But she is a shadow beside my father, a subtle firmament, a song without words. She was beautiful once.

—Describe your father.

Physically, a squat and stringy man, a peasant's build, muscles in the calves and lower arms. A few clumps of grayish hair around a fist-sized sunburn at the top of the head. Eyes like blue stones. A buttressed nose. Lips in an expression of disgust. One silver tooth, a wedding band too small for his finger; dark, leathery hands with plenty of callus. Alligator shirts and a belt buckle with his initials, RJS.

—His interior is undoubtedly more complex.

Undoubtedly.

—And is this the heart of our conversation? The very center?

My father, yes.

—Discuss the reasons you resent his presence.

At the age of five, for yelling at me to be quiet when I hadn't been talking. At the age of seven, for standing beside me while I played the piano, humming the tune as it should have been played. At the age of ten, for accusing me of lying when I actually *was* lying. At the age of fifteen, for refusing to notice me. For coming home from work in his steel-tipped shoes, ignoring my face and my ideas.

—Your age at present?

Twenty-eight.

—Answer the following question as truthfully as possible. Why did you lie to your father and how often did you do so?

On all occasions and in any climate. On the boardwalk in Ocean City, New Jersey, over a slice of pizza allegedly purchased only forty minutes before supper. In his bedroom in Wilmington, regarding a centipede found flattened against the wall with a black-soled shoe. On the eve of my departure for college, in reference to issues of virginity. At the burial of my dog, Woofer, when asked if I was sad. I always refuse to be sad in his presence, as he refuses to be in mine.

—For this you are firmly set against him, and can't forgive. Is that the essence of our talk?

Quintessence.

—Let's begin at the beginning. Was he present at your birth?

Pacing the waiting room, fatherly, a sliding grin below his nose. I was fifth in a line of daughters, a last resort.

—What did he bring with him?

To the hospital, a cribbage board, intended to entertain my mother in the labor room. To my existence, a series of longings and a vague dissatisfaction, a love of graveyards and a need for affection greater than that he was willing to supply.

—Is this common among Germans?

Cribbage? No, their game is pinochle, mainly—but, my mother being English, this would have seemed inappropriate, cumbrous, a legacy intended to warp the card-playing future of the eager fetus.

—Tell me about your ancestors.

On one side, Lady Godiva and the Knights of Templar, a long line of bookworms and opera buffs, even a great-grand-mother nicknamed "Mother of Israel" for bearing twelve sons. On the other side, a group of scrappy immigrants from Leip-zig, old women who refused to allow their husbands a mo-ment's peace.

—Describe your childhood.

We lived in Wilmington, Delaware. In the house I grew up in, there was a bathroom with three sinks, a shower, and two identical toilets side by side. My father designed it with special allowances for pipes and plumbing, so that all three sinks and the tub could be running water, and the toilets could flush simultaneously. It was a joy to watch, and when my sisters and I were children, we often brought our friends to see the bath-room, where, on the count of three, we pushed the handles and turned the small glass knobs and listened to the glory of the water all around us.

—Is that all?

It was the root of my father's frustrations. Despite the matching toilet-paper fixtures, the six-foot mirror above the sinks, the standing towel rack with fifteen arms, none of the five of his daughters agreed to use the room together. In-tensely private, we lined up quietly outside, taking our turns and making sure to lock the door behind us. Except for the watery exhibitions, we used the bathroom one by one.

—When you were seven, you took a walk and lost your way. A policeman brought you back in his patrol car, and there was your father, raking leaves in the side yard. What were his words on this occasion?

Where the hell have you been? We didn't know you were missing.

—Several years later, he was standing in the very same spot when you rode your bicycle down the hill and into the driveway, obstinately refusing to use the brakes because your sister had dared you not to use them, and slammed into the lamppost, landing face down in the pachysandra. What did he say?

He said, *What in God's name do you think you're doing, Julie?*

—You have always resented him. Where does your anger come from?

Not from raw dislike and not from distaste. The best of me was born from him, his love of stories. His unhesitating lies.

—What type of lies?

Of grandparents stronger than they were in fact, of people he wished he knew but never met. He is a tale-teller at heart. He used to creep into my room and pluck the night-light from the wall; it was darker than ink, he'd drop it deep in his jacket pocket and sit in the rocker at the edge of the room. He'd prop his feet on the end of my bed and tell stories, bloody adventures about men stranded at sea without medicine (one of them removed his own appendix without anesthesia; another tore out his own tonsils, gazing at his terrified face in a full-size mirror), or science-fiction tales of black clouds covering the sun, comets barely missing the earth in yearly orbits, exploding stars. *We're so small,* he used to say. Then he'd walk out the door.

—His love of science is what bothers you. It makes you jealous.

Superfluous more than jealous. Redundant. Infinitesimal. I was the worst of his pupils, confusing neutrons with protons, the laws of gravity with laws of friction. The quadratic equation slid through the warm blue ropes of my cerebrum, remaining buried there, wasting space.

—Once, as a teenager, you stood poised outside his bedroom door in the middle of the night, listening.

True, I stood by the door hoping he would open it, allow me to confess to things I hadn't done, a whole childhood full of wrongdoing and imagination. I hoped he would fling wide the door in his striped pajamas, arms open but eyes half shut, and ask me what I had done.

—Were you guilty?

As most offspring are, guilty of craving his attention in any form, capable of sex and other theatrics to win his notice, his bald eye roving the crevasse of my life.

—Your father is an old man growing older. He dreams of death in all its forms.

Both of us do. I dream of the end of the world as my father's face rising over the side of the earth instead of the sun. He dreams of hospitals, nursing homes, IV tubes, enemas given by young black women.

—And you refuse to forgive him?

Not for the anger, but for the love.

—What about love? He never offered it?

Never named it, mentioned it, spoke it out loud.

—Not in twenty-eight years?

Not in my life. Seldom in his.

—Describe his attitude toward tears.

In the middle of an argument, he once said: *Crying is justified only in the event of the death of a healthy child.*

—Do you ever attempt to see things his way?

Not really, not to any great extent, not at all. He thinks that anything can be explained, that anything studied long enough can be understood.

—And your attitude is the opposite?

That almost nothing has a reasonable explanation, that the longer a thing is studied, the more abstract it will become. But my father explains the origins of air, the earth's ingredients and measure. He describes the solar system as a raisin crumb cake: the raisins are planets, the doughy mass a universe of sky. The cake will bake and the raisins will rise . . .

—What does he fear?

Dissipation and waste. The separation of matter into spheres, the undoing of those spheres, the inevitable movement from order to disorder. He searches day and night for a special logic to destruction, a pattern for all unreason, an explanation for chaos. And only in the darkest moments does he sense a tiny crack, a hairline fissure through which his knowledge, like a clever gas, escapes when he isn't looking. Vulnerability rushes in to take its place.

—Is this chaos?

A related phenomenon, chaos being its counterweight, its nearest neighbor. The degradation of energy. The tendency of small, otherwise reasonable forces to disagree and move away, traveling in centrifugal directions.

—If your father were a comet moving away from the earth in a centrifugal direction, what would you be?

A net of stars, result of some unknown explosion, scattered across the frying pan of night above his head; a warm illusion, white filament, ignoring him as he rumbled toward the edge of my dispersion, looking right and then left with his round comet eyes, his blue-gray craters.

—Earlier you said your father was an amateur scientist. Is he also an amateur stargazer?

A man of many hats. Physicist, businessman, star man, hat man.

—On the eve of your marriage, you telephoned your father from the business phone downstairs. He answered in the bedroom but said nothing, and you both held on to the phone in silence. Was that cruelty on his part or yours?

. . .

—We still don't seem to be covering this question of resentment. Even the grandchildren have forgiven him.

True, they play in his lap. He is accepted, pardoned. He

carves the roast at the head of the table, doling patriarchal slices thin and thick on the point of his knife. They pardon him for his age and for his stature. He is guiltless at the head of the table, therefore irresponsible, irredeemable.

—Does it make you uncomfortable to be incapable of forgiveness?

He ignored me. He compared me to others. He refused to encourage me. He held no ambition for my sake.

—You once admired him. What did you want to be when you grew up?

His shadow. His bodyguard. His idol.

—Will he forgive you?

Always and without regret. Crossing his hands behind his neck and leaning backward in his chair.

—You aren't asking his forgiveness, but he grants it, anyway. If you forgave him in his turn, what would you say?

I take back everything I've said. **Q**

[1]

The thing I really want to tell you about is my father and the way he was always on the run on those feet, but the thing is that I don't know what to do with him once I get him on the page, and I'm not all that sure I will be able to get him on the page in the first place anyway, and then if I do somehow by hook or by crook manage to get even one little bit of him, even one little aspect of him down on the page, I'm not all that sure I can keep even that little bit of him there for long enough to do any of us any good at all, even if I do figure out something to do with him once I get him there, because, you see, everything would have to be just right, just exactly perfectly right, and it would have to stay that way, because the instant that everything wasn't just exactly perfectly right, then he would be gone just like that. Instantaneously. Absolutely. Irrevocably. Gone. Just like that. Because my father would not, he absolutely would not under any circumstances just sit around passively for the purposes of politeness or anything else and just tolerate things being less than perfectly just right. No, he would get right out of there and fast, and lots of times before he got right out of there he would just break things— just whatever things happened to be around—to show exactly how he felt about it—he would crash things to the ground so there would be absolutely no doubt as to where he stood on the matter, whatever the matter might be, because where and how he stood was an important issue for my father—or he would hack things into pieces or just destroy things utterly in one way or another and then fling them, just hurl them away from himself and out into the abyss of intolerable imperfections out there orbiting aimlessly, forever banished from his awareness and from his sight. And if he couldn't hurl the

things away from himself, then he would hurl himself away
from the things that weren't just right and out of the scene at
hand right that instant, right that very moment, as though he
might almost will himself magically into another universe.
Like, for example, it might be that a friend of his whom he had
known for thirty years and whom he might have thought was
a lot like himself, since they had gone to high school together,
or it might be that they had both spent the war in hospitals or
something like that, and it might be that my father and this
friend of his would be sitting in a country-club dining room
with starched white tablecloths or even in a café on the border
with Mexican waiters in aprons standing around, and this
friend might just inadvertently say something that might strike
my father as indicating a fundamental breach of some kind, or
maybe he would think it indicated some sort of betrayal or
personal insult, as he was constantly on the alert for indica-
tions of these kinds, and then my father would just shoot from
his chair, knocking it backward, would throw the wooden table
with all its cutlery and crystal to the floor, and then my father
would just run, would just go charging out of the room as fast
as he possibly could in that stiff-legged walk he had, and then
he might never speak to that old friend of his again, just to
show that that was how strongly he felt about it. And suffering
the consequences of showing how he felt about it was something that it seemed to me he didn't mind doing, and the fact
that people didn't know what to do with him or how to handle
the situations that he would cause didn't seem to bother him,
as if that was something that was just in his body, as if the way
he lived in his body was such that he had to show and act out
everything. As if that was just a fact of reality and what other
people chose to do about it was their own affair. Even when
he was sitting in a chair, his fingers would be running and
tapping and drumming to the rhythm of something inside him.

I remember looking at his left hand one day, the way you
would look at the hand of a stranger on the subway—secretly
spying on the hand while the stranger was looking in another

direction—stealthily I was observing that small innocent creature—my father's left hand with its short fingers, the small
clean nails, the pink skin with the brown freckles across the
back. He had small hands for a man of his size—people used
to say that when he was young and would get into fights his
small hands were a problem for him. His hands looked to me
like a boy's hands. They seemed to belong to someone I didn't
know, not the person that we would all be so afraid of when
he came home from work on a bad day and came charging into
the house from the garage and we would all be sitting or
standing around in the kitchen or the den and we would
have known from the way we'd heard his car hit the driveway
and by the speed with which he would have made it to the
back door in that not-exactly-limping-but-making-lurching-for-
ward-look-purposeful walk we all three grew up imitating—we
would know, we would just know the way you know when you
swing a bat that this one's going to be a foul, and even though
the bat hasn't even hit the ball yet, you know that it's too late
already to change it and that there is nothing you can do,
because it's all already in motion and this one is just going to
be a foul. And that's mostly the way it would be with him—all
you could do would be to just try to get out of the way in time,
because when things weren't just right, sometimes he would
fall down, because he had those bad feet, but usually he would
just break things, like he would break ashtrays and dishes and
glasses and chairs and windows and doors and locks on doors
and just anything—he even broke his own bones a lot. Sometimes if my mother fixed dinner and everything wasn't just
right, he would throw the corncobs on the floor, because there
was no plate set out for them the way he wanted, or he would
hurl a whole tomato aspic across the room, because he had to
have something to chew on. But mostly my father liked to eat
better than he liked most things. He would lunge into each bite
of food as he ate, surrounding and attacking each forkful as
though the act of taking a bite were an act of capture, and as
he ate he would go faster and faster, as though accelerating

toward some climactic moment, and sometimes as he did so, his eyes would seem to glaze, as though he were not only consuming but also being consumed, merging with something larger in which to be lost the way he told me one time he was lost in the morphine they gave him when his feet were crushed in the first place and he spent years in hospitals like the one at Valley Forge, where I saw him for the first time I can remember seeing him and knowing that he was my father, and he was all bound up in a cast that covered his whole body, and I heard he later cut that cast off himself and went running around like he wasn't supposed to do, and he hurt himself, and they didn't know what to do with him and they had to put him in a new cast. He was always hurting himself, but he didn't seem to care about that, because he wanted to have things a certain way. Like when they operated on his feet the first time and he wouldn't have a general anesthetic, because they wouldn't promise him that they wouldn't cut off the worse of the feet, because they said he would never walk on them because of the pain, but he wouldn't let them do it, and so after that he made himself walk, but the feet were always hurting—especially that one worse foot—and he was constantly moving them, like if we would go to a movie, he wouldn't just sit there but he would be up and down and up and down the whole time, getting popcorn and drinks and going to the bathroom and just walking around, and while he was sitting there in his seat, his feet would be moving up and down in the aisle, or his knees would be going back and forth and back and forth, and lots of times something in the movie wouldn't be just right, so we would all have to get up and leave right in the middle. Even when he was sitting at home and watching TV, it would be the same way. He would be moving his feet up and down the whole time, pumping them up and down and back and forth in those dark brown, lace-up, oxford-type shoes. The shoes would always have to be of the softest leather, and always the best and sometimes handmade, and they must have been a lot of trouble to find, because one of his feet was a different size and shape than the other foot since the war, so he usually had to either buy two pairs—one for one foot and one for the other— or he had to have them specially made to measure, but then his feet hurt all the time anyway. He would keep on moving those feet up and down and back and forth, and they were so stiff and so square that they looked almost like wooden feet, and he walked on them and used them in a way that seemed to me to be just as if they were wooden feet, because the ankles didn't move, so they had this stiff look, and if you could see them without shoes and without those thin dress socks he would always wear, then you would see how stiff and wasted and white and woodish they appeared, and why he walked on them as if he were walking on stilts—except that in a way they were stilts that had been fashioned in the early days of plastic surgery and were made of bone and flesh and also nerves, with those pink raised scars all around the tendons and the square heels and the ankles, which were bony and lumpy in an un-defined sort of way—like man-made approximations of feet. And his feet were always getting injured and reinjured, like the time when my parents went to Nassau with their friends and my father didn't believe them when they said there were sting-ing sea urchins on the beach, and so he wound up with a swollen foot full of stinging sea-urchin quills, as well as with a bad sunburn, because he also didn't believe that he couldn't stay out in the sun as long as anyone with his redhead's skin, and so the next day he was stuck in his hotel room while everyone else was out on the beach again, and he didn't know what to do with himself all day, and he got curious about the little metal trapdoor that was in the ceiling of the bathroom of his hotel room, so he found a screwdriver and undid all four screws and the metal trapdoor fell corner-down right on the instep of his now triply injured foot, so he wound up in an-other hospital.

I remember when they came back from that trip and he was so angry and breaking things every day, and he paced up and down the kitchen on one cane and ate three whole packages of Nestle's cooking chocolate, and when he did that, he got this look on his face that I remembered seeing when I was a very small child and I saw him pull a bottle out of the wood-bin that was in the brick fireplace, and he turned that bottle up, and as he drank, he lunged toward that bottle with his face—he lunged into it as though he were Alice plunging in that instant through some looking-glass boundary in his own mind, and his face seemed to me to have the look of standing in a strong wind. And it was way back then when I was small that things were the worst with the drinking and with the feet, like during the time when he was in the leg casts and he couldn't get around except on heavy wooden crutches, so there wasn't much he could do except make models of boats and planes and tanks and things, and there was this one model boat he was working on for a long time, and he would sit for hours absorbed in working on it and not moving very much at all, and it was a good one made of balsa wood, and then one day there was a piece he couldn't find and the boat was almost finished and he couldn't get that piece and he couldn't get it and he couldn't get anyone else to get it right that minute, and he got so mad that he just took his crutch and smashed that model boat into bits and pieces, and then it was ruined, and he had really liked that boat too and had been working on it for a long time and had bought the dope to paint it with and it was going to be blue and gray and red, and I had helped him to pick out the colors, but then he had crunched it into lots of pieces and it couldn't be put back together, and he had ruined everything. I didn't want to talk to him much for a long time after that, which made him even madder.

After the casts came off, he went from the crutches to using two canes, and his feet hurt a lot then and he had a hard time learning to balance on those two canes and would fall down a lot, such as the time when he had the two canes and it was dark and it was raining and the car lights and the street-lights were shiny on the pavement like streaky-colored mirrors, and we were all hurrying, and my mother said to him,

Don't cross now, you'll fall. And the look he gave her, I thought he was going to hit her, but instead he leaned on those two thin canes with all his weight and he lunged into the street, and it was raining hard and there were cars, and he went thumping across as fast as he could, and he went lurching across as well as he could, but his weight was on those two thin cane tips, and one slid out from under him and he fell down hard, slipping and sliding in the street, and cars screeched and skidded on the mirrored wet pavement, and he glared right into their grills, baring his teeth and yelling and cursing, and then he looked back at my mother and me as if we were the same as the car grills, and then he struggled up, saying not to help him, goddammit, and to get away from him, and then he hit at the car nearest with one of the canes, and then he took off his nice new overcoat, which was now all wet and grease-stained, and he threw it in the street, and then he was mad and wouldn't talk to anyone for the rest of the night. I was getting to where I didn't want to talk to him all that much either, and not too long after that, when it was my fifth or sixth birthday, he gave me a pair of tall wooden stilts, and he made a point of saying that I had to learn to use them all by myself, but I never did, and I can still see those red-and-green-painted stilts leaning reproachfully against the back wall of the garage—and then months and even years later he would once in a while get this look in his eye, and he would ask me why I never learned to use those stilts.

After that, he went back to the surgeons and said that he had changed his mind and that he wanted them to go ahead and amputate that one of those feet that was always hurting him the most, but at that point he could already walk, so they refused to do it, and so he had to live with himself like that. Sometimes that one worse foot would bother him so much that he would go back to using one crutch around the house, just for a week or two. During one of the times while he was doing this and I was about five or six and I didn't want to go to school and was hiding out in the back yard hoping they would just forget about me for long enough that I could skip school for just that one day, and my mother was yelling around the house for me and was getting mad, and finally she started yelling out the back door for me, and then my father came clumping out, still in his bathrobe and on that one crutch, and he was furious that I would dare to defy them like that. I realized that I had made a big mistake, and I hunched down behind the newly cut woodpile, hoping that he wouldn't see me, but after calling out a couple of times, he headed straight for me, and I could see him through the spaces between the stacked logs near the top of the pile, and I was looking around for an escape, and then his crutch sank into the ground and he fell. He fell heavily, right into some uncut branches, and scraped his hand and arm. If I lifted up just a little, I could see him through the woodpile furiously struggling with his legs and feet and with his bath-robe and the crutch, and his face turning redder and redder, and then he picked up a hatchet that had been left by the uncut wood and he started hitting at his crutch with it. He got up on his one knee and hacked and hacked at that crutch, and he was chopping it in two. And I hunched down low behind the wood-pile, and he just kept on hacking and hacking and hacking, and it seemed as if he had forgotten about me and about the yard and even about the crutch and everything, and that all he was thinking about was the hacking that went on and on, and then there was another sound—a worrying, whining sound that was deep and desperate, like the sound of an animal trying to get out of a trap, and it went on and on, and there was no other place for me to hide, and then everything stopped. Suddenly all the sounds stopped. I got up slowly to where I could peer between the logs and see him, and I could see that he had stopped hacking and was looking at the foot that was right there in front of him—it was the worse one of the two, and he was just staring at that foot with that hatchet in his hand, and that was when I knew that I had to get out of there right that minute, and so I jumped up and ran out from behind the woodpile and across the yard, and that was when my father looked up and saw me.

[2]

I think I'd have to say that the main thing about my mother was her hair. It was long and long, down to her waist, and that's where she trimmed it off even, and then she braided it. And then she twisted it and she coiled it and she pinned it up against the back of her neck. And my mother's hair was dark like mine is, but it was fine and silky and smooth against her head, not dense and wiry and full of cowlicks like mine is.

And she wore it long like that always, right through times when long hair was not in style—and my mother was a very stylish woman. She wore it long when everyone else had cut theirs and kept on cutting theirs—right through all the pompadours and pageboys and poodle cuts. Right through the bubbles and flips and everything else, she just kept on braiding that long braid and then wrapping it around and around in back and pinning it with those oversized black-wire hairpins. And then anchoring it with those giant tortoiseshell hairpins, almost as if that coil were holding herself and all of us in place as well as the hair. No matter what was being done, my mother just went right on doing what she had always done and knowing that it was the best.

And it was the perfect thing on her, because she had a face of greater evenness on the two sides than any I have ever seen—she appeared to have almost perfect symmetry. And she had that high wide smoothly rounded forehead that came square to the hairline, where the hair flared gently away before being pulled back into the inevitable coiled braid. She had that high smooth inscrutable forehead that demanded hair with seriousness, hair with innocence, hair with all the serenity that hair can ever have.

And she would always wear it up. She would never not wear it up like that. Maybe "never" is not true, but it seemed that way. And her hair was always neat—if any ends were pulled loose by too vigorous an action or were blown loose by a wind of greater force and roughness than any my mother had ever intended to be exposed to, then those ends would be tucked in again. Sometimes the hair would be taken down and recombed. When she took it down, she would pull the hairpins out with one hand moving rapidly, searching and gathering and removing pins and placing them hurriedly on the dresser, and with the other hand she would hold together and manipulate the coiled braid until it was ready to come down. Then, when the braid came down, she would remove the tight rubber band and start running her fingers through the braid, separating and undoing it. And then she would brush it out upside down.

I can still see her hands braiding that long, thick braid, her body leaning to one side, head tilted over, she and I both watching that one braid lengthening in the mirror, her fingers moving in and out in that particular dance that produced the braid, bit by bit, holding and adding on, holding on and adding, and then tying it off, winding up the end with a tight rubber band—making the end into a stubby hairy little nub that would be tucked underneath and never seen, so that the circle of braid at the back of her head would appear to be infinitely continuous—with no beginning and no end.

I would often sit on the edge of my mother's bathtub and watch her and watch her as she would brush out her hair until it would crackle with electricity, and then divide it and smooth it and start making the braid. The bathroom would smell of lotion and face powder and of the smell that her hair had when she brushed it out like that, and sometimes I would help with a strap or a hairpin, and I would study the way she went through all the motions exactly the same way every time, looking for the clues on how to be a woman, but looking in the mirror, I could not help observing how small and graceful and smooth my mother appeared, and how tall and clumsy and red-faced I was, looking back at myself with dismay, hair flying in all directions.

Then, when the braid went up, her face would go through a subtle change of a nature I cannot describe, except to say that her neck would seem to elongate and in that moment it would seem to me that she was as self-sufficient as a cat. She seemed to me to have a secret with herself that no one else could ever share, a secret that lived in the house with us but that would only once in a while be glimpsed, and then only out of the corner of your eye—you could almost swear a shape was there, but when you looked directly at it, there would be only a blankness, an empty space.

My mother could braid so fast and with such deftness and control that it seemed to me she could have done it in her sleep—could have done it without noticing what she was doing. In fact, she braided not only her own hair but also mine and that of my next-in-age sister—the three of us every single morning and again at night if it needed to be recombed for some social event. We children wore French braids when we were little. French braids are braids which start small, with a small amount of hair on the sides of your forehead, and then, as they are woven closely down on your head, more and more strands are added in a gradual accumulation, until every hair on your head is caught up into these two tight ridges running from front to back on both sides, all the way down your head, and then the two pigtail extensions stick out behind your ears. Ours would be braided so tightly that they would curl back toward the front, and our scalps were tough, even later after our hair was cut short. My mother went to a lot of trouble to keep all the hair in the family under control. She did not tolerate any flyaway hair or messy hair or hair in the face. She would often ask me if her own hair had any strands escaping or hairpins slipping out of place, and it was part of my position as the oldest to help keep an eye on this for her, as well as on the same situation with my younger sister.

Once in a while, when I was still small enough to feel close to the ground, I would come across a long, single hair that had somehow escaped with its full length and would be lying curled around and around itself unnoticed, black and spidery on the white bathroom tile. I would pick it up and hold it up and marvel at its length and its singleness, and once, knowing how much effort was expended to keep them disposed of, I kept one of these escaped hairs. It seemed to me that it was a particularly long and heavy one, and it had a kink down toward one end that must have been caused by some rubber band or bobby pin. I wound it up on my finger and then put it in my little box of found objects, which for one reason or another I felt had to be kept. And then I hid the box, because I knew she would throw it away if she found it, because she kept the house neat and clean.

Just the same as with her hair. Except for rare occasions, or when she was combing it or washing it, we rarely saw my mother's hair down. Living with her, you wouldn't really have the sense of being around someone who had all that hair, because it was always done up and always the same. I suppose "always" is not exactly the right thing to say. I remember once when she had been washing her hair and had to pick me up from school before it was dry, and when I got in the car with my books and saw that long black tangled wet hair streaming over the back of the seat like some strange animal, I was horrified. I couldn't stop looking at that hair and at her, and I was afraid some of my friends might see it—somehow it seemed to me to be something indecent. She laughed at me and gave me a funny look, and she told me that when I was still in a crib she had once leaned over to pick me up with her hair wet and loose, and it fell sudden and dark across the crib and I wouldn't stop screaming for an hour after that.

Another time, for a grade-school fair, my mother dressed as a fortune-telling gypsy and wore her hair down and around her shoulders like smoke, and lots of veils and bangles and things, and with her dark eyes and pierced ears, she really did look the part. I would keep walking past her booth and looking and looking at her, and she would call out to me to come in and have my fortune told, and I would just walk past. She had it dark in the booth, with candles, and it looked as if her hair were moving behind her as the candles flickered, and every time I would walk past, she would call out again, and I don't know why, but I didn't want her telling my fortune—I just wanted to look at her again and again without her seeing me doing it. But she was always seeing me. It seemed to me that there was never a time when she wasn't seeing me before I could see her.

Another time, when I was about thirteen, they went to a big party where everyone was supposed to dress Hawaiian, and she told me that after dinner she needed my help getting dressed. Like always when my parents went out, there was this atmosphere of bustling and subdued excitement, and whiffs of perfume all around the house. In her bathroom-dressing room the air would be humid from the bath she would have just taken, and heavily scented from all the oils and lotions and makeup that would be opened and used during the course of the preparations. She and I could see and talk to each other's reflection in the long, foggy mirror over the dressing table in which her face would be lit as if on stage, and mine would be dimmer and behind hers—a watcher and an assistant.

She had gotten a grass skirt somewhere and had strung masses of flowers together and had also bought a dozen bottles of Touch & Glow suntan-color makeup, because she didn't have time to get a deep tan. I was to help with putting this makeup on her back and where she couldn't reach.

Her skin was so white against the black hair. It was an opaque kind of gardenia-white, not transparent and blotchy like mine. The whiteness of her skin as she stood there in the bathroom in her underpants made her seem all the more naked, and as I smoothed the orangy-tan makeup on her back and shoulders—being careful not to get any in her hair—and then on her legs, I felt funny, because ordinarily there wasn't that much touching between us, and because it seemed to me that my mother's nakedness was being covered by the makeup and yet uncovered at the same time. She had made up her face and neck and arms, and the color change had transformed her curving, compact, almost-Oriental face and body into something tawny and muscular. She put on the grass skirt, and then my mother let her hair down. She bent over with the hair, brushing it and brushing it until it seemed to be moving of its own will and the bathroom was filled with its particular animal smell. Then she straightened up and shook out the now flying mane, letting it fall around her shoulders and down her back, moving now with a kind of power that was a loud music to which the hair swayed and bounced as she moved. It seemed to be breathing. She looked at herself in the mirror with an expression I had never seen before, and I stood back in the shadows to watch my mother. **Q**

Jim took him a powerful excitement when I told him about the aborted newborns that they was all up and a-blowing about and trying to get put cease and desisted. Jim right off took like he knew the whole of it without knowing not a particle on it that was true, as some niggers are like to up and take on, and he came out and said:

"Why, Mr. Huck, if that ain't the dad-foolishest thing I ever did run me across, then I be a white gentleman like yourself, bless you, child"—giving me a hug—"for there ain't no call for to risk killing you a whole woman when a body could just wait on for her to have the baby and then shoot it."

No doubt, you can tell right out from the top that Jim is a nigger gone and said some tolerable reemy truck, so I done my dosest to out and rid him of them nothing ideas.

I said: "I reckon I ain't never before heard such nonsense as them things you just gone and said. Now, don't it seem apparent to a body with sense in it that if they shoot the baby after the mother had gone and had it out, then that would be the same as murdering another living creature?"

Jim has the weakest morals when he wants to of any nigger I ever laid eyes on; he scarce hardly waited for them words to get clear out of my mouth ere he was insisting on all feather of daffness.

He said: "Mr. Huck, if you go and shoot on an unprotected number of womens, you be like murdering—ain't that so? And if you miss their babies and abort the womens, you done murdered—ain't that so? But if you was to use your volumes of smarts and set for a piece and figure on it, Heaven love you, child"—he petted me—"and figure on out a ways, you'd see that it done far better to shoot the little thing without all the obfuscation of the mammy in the way—ain't that so?"

And you can imagine, when I heard this stuff, I took on tolerable sicklike to know that I had befriended me a nigger what didn't know the difference between murdering a body and aborting on it, which is kin to not knowing the difference between right and wrong. And then I got to thinking, and thought that I had already gotten all set to go and burn in Hell. But I reckoned that Jim most likely wanted to go to Heaven, as long as they would let him in, so I decided to put my head down on this one and try to make Jim see the light—so he wouldn't look plumb foolish in the Hereafter.

"Why, Jim, don't you own a single iota of rationalness? An abortion is one of them operations and there's doctors what can do them lickety-split-like and wouldn't miss the baby on no count from that range, and don't hardly never hurt its mother."

But Jim had got his woolly head all fixed on this one and weren't about to listen to no sense from me. Instead, he got himself even more powerful sweaty and started up like he was a nickel away from busting out and cussing. I never did see such an ornery nigger as when Jim gets his mind on to something.

Jim said: "But, Lord preserve you, honey"—he clasped me up—"how's the doctor to hit the baby without shooting through the poor thing's mammy? It sure would take a power of skill for a body to shoot around the mother. And don't it occur to you a piece that aborting them women's babies is a fool waste of them babies, anyway?"

I allowed that if a nigger was so set on his opinion, then there weren't no way to help on no count, so I didn't up and try to explain all the reams of stuff that Jim wasn't seeing correctly—like them facts like the doctor have to shoot straight through the thing's mother, otherwise it wouldn't be a real upstanding operation; and also them things about the baby being a waste to up and abort with, it being right clear that some babies is good and others isn't. **Q**

Sons take me to breakfast at the Pump Room. They like to be seen in such places. I do, too. Wear my silver Michael Jackson coat with matching silver dress cut to waist. Tuck a pink silk scarf in the cleavage. Kelly and David are commodity traders. David is a runner in the pits at the Chicago Board of Trade. Kelly works with computers and carries a Quotron, little machine that gives constant prices on commodities. They steal money from farmers. Don't care what anybody says that is the truth. Played Mozart to them in their cribs. Read Shakespeare at bedtime. Told them about Gandhi before Gandhi was invented. Worked in Kennedy and Stevenson campaign offices wearing Kelly in a sling on my back. Their babysitters all belonged to SDS. Nothing took. They talk only of money. Talk in terms of millions. They will make me buy breakfast. They look around the room for important people. Only tourists, people who pay sixty-nine dollars for the weekend and ride in the horse carriages. Sorry I wasted my silver outfit. Already frayed. Sons count my drinks and my cigarettes. Don't know why they want to preserve me. We have nothing in common. "You're my first drafts," I say, "want to tear you up and do a rewrite." With new babies, I will be strict and religious, throw out my silver dress, have a locked room with forbidden books. They would turn out the way I wanted. Walk the few blocks home. Gray gloomy Sunday in Chicago. Nothing new. Would go home and play Billie Holiday record of same name. Thought that universal parent thought, my children, what I could have done different. When Kelly and David were eight and ten, we sold car mats to Mexicans at the Maxwell Street Market. My husband bought a warehouse filled with seconds from a bankrupt rubber company. Early Sunday mornings we loaded the trunk and back seat of our car with blue and red car mats, then drove to the market. Some days we made nine hundred dollars. Late afternoon, while I drove home, boys sat on remaining car mats in backseat, happily counting dirty dollar bills. Threw dollars in the air, sang, grabbed them with their dirty little fists. Took to the market much better than to Mozart. When we ran out of car mats, we sold anything— jewelry, junk, old clothes. When boys were in high school, took them to Europe. Read all those dumb books about cultural advantages. Books written about other people's children. Meet a race-car driver in Paris who teaches boys how to drive. In Florence, David never leaves the hotel, sits on balcony spying on hookers with high-powered binoculars. Counts the money, the men, the hours hookers work. "If I see another church I'll puke," he says to me when I beg him to come with me to the Duomo. Kelly buys switchblade and hangs around the straw market with vendors, helps them sell little plastic Pietàs. I sit in the Duomo and cry. See some nuns. "Take me with you," I say, "I am almost a virgin. I have never had any children." Now this gloomy Sunday, more past than present, let myself in apartment. Sixty-fourth floor, wrapped in gray clouds. Was glad. Didn't want to watch life out the windows. If this is heaven, it's spacious and empty. Two long black couches face wall, two naked mannequins sit on coffee table. Bought in a junk shop. Named them when I got them, but can't remember their names. A few months ago, sons call me, singing, "We're makin' money on the meltdown! We're makin' money on the meltdown!" Want to write a musical comedy. Can see dancers and hear music. Wild colors like lava flows. *Springtime in Germany.* Only better. Maybe Julie Andrews as lead. Maybe me. Take off my silver dress. Not for house. Only for party. Put dress on mannequin. Mannequin falls over. **Q**

President
Soft-Tuch Paper
112 Grand Street
Barnes, Iowa 40986   June 6

Dear Sir:

The toilet paper, the cover says "225 Sq. Ft. Total Area,
400 2-ply sheets." I got here a roll was okay two-ply but 396
sheets, a whole day it took. So missing from what? a hundred
million? rolls a year, big bucks you are robbing the American
public! I am old man not so good shape.

So?

Yrs. truly,
Irv Miller

SOFT-TUCH PAPER PRODUCTS 112 Grand Street Barnes, Iowa
40986

Mr. Irving Miller
28430 Bellon Boulevard
Chicago, Illinois 09856   June 20

Dear Mr. Miller:

Your June 6th letter was directed to Mr. Edgar Korman,
our Vice President for Public Relations, who has passed it on
to me.

You will suppose me, Mr. Miller, to be a relatively minor
figure in the Soft-Tuch corporate hierarchy. This is indeed the
case. I am one of a group of five retained to protect, to enhance
if possible, the Soft-Tuch image. It falls to us to respond, in

Mr. Korman's phrase, to "the little people everywhere" who have reached out to this giant corporation.

This is a perfectly terrible job. It has cost me my self-esteem, Mr. Miller. It has exhausted my patience with the multitude of aging and/or demented layabouts whose petty plaints are in reality of no concern whatsoever to the Soft-Tuch Company.

I sit here in my little cubicle, your four-sheets-short protest before me. The clock ticks. My life is passing . . .

The facts, Mr. Miller, are these. We sell millions and millions of rolls of Soft-Tuch Toilet Tissue annually, each roll promising 400 sheets. Not so. We provide only 395 sheets. (Your 396-sheeter, a production slip, is what we call a "biggie.") The extra money resulting from our deceit supplies booze and hookers to the Soft-Tuch Board of Directors.

Please write again if you have other questions.

> Sincerely,
> Roger Maxwell
> Consumer Relations

Mr. Edgar Korman
Vice President
Soft-Tuch Paper
112 Grand Street
Barnes, Iowa 40986   June 24

Dear Korman:

Some company you got! I wrote before, copy attached, today comes this Maxwell, a smart-ass letter you wouldn't believe I didn't give also a copy attached.

The media should only know! *Sixty Minutes* for sure would take such a story. An old Jewish man, a senior with bad health, insults he gets from crooks, a big company? Look out! Any minute, a knock on the door! Open, there is Mike Wallace, maybe also the big shvartzer with the beard!

I am also blind almost, and like a pretzel bent.
So?

Yrs. truly,
Irv Miller

Mr. Irving Miller
28430 Bellon Boulevard
Chicago, Illinois 09856   July 2

Dear Mr. Miller:

Your letter of June 24th, with enclosures, has been read with great interest here. Mr. Maxwell is no longer in our employ, and I apologize for the misguided jests—as I'm sure you are aware—contained in his letter to you.

Our production department advises as follows: Soft-Tuch Toilet Tissue rolls are produced by a "continuous band" process, with the severing blade set to create a 400-sheet roll, with a consumer protection margin of from +three to +six sheets. This provides a roll containing three to six more sheets than the label indicates. If you have already communicated with any media regarding our sheet count, kindly make available to such media the information contained herein.

A complimentary carton of Soft-Tuch Toilet Tissue (100 rolls) has been express-shipped to you today.

Sincerely,
Edgar Korman
Vice President

Mr. Ed Korman
Soft-Tuch Paper
112 Grand Street
Barnes, Iowa 40986   July 8

Korman!

All I got wrong with me, the bowels, swelling, I got no strength to lift 100 rolls arrived today, a box like a house. One roll I took inside the bathroom to give a count. Comes the outside paper off, from the middle jumps out a black spider and bites my peniss. Your production dept can again explain? Your lawyer also should write. From mine you will hear soon, believe me. Also *Sixty Minutes*.

Yrs. truly,
Irv Miller **Q**

Never more interested in the tintinnabulations of the world in your ears than at this time. With this deadness you have in your fingertips, with your shortness of breath, with what, if pressed, you would term your lost youth, you have come into your inherited madnesses—birds chattering in Greek, radio broadcasts from those who have passed away, streets resurfaced as trampolines, religious significances in the smallest things. Still, you manage to doubt your twinges of doubt.

And to listen to fluctuating pulses—you imagine that this will occupy a portion of the afternoon and evening—to lick off her lipstick smears, to press the flesh, breathe deep halitotic fumes, be revivified, if in a less vigorous incarnation. It's simple stuff. Get your hands dirty. Wake up and smell the coffee. Let sleeping dogs lie.

Yet symptoms do not pass so easily. This is the time when, hunched over a ream box of hieroglyphics written by an Alabamian dwarf in which the bloody dental plates and whittlings of his recollections are presented as if under glass, while you are squinting and scratching the scar on your earlobe, while counting comma splices, just now, you receive from the large office at the end of the hall, by hand, a letter to type. A personal letter, and it has Ogden Aspern's address at the top.

It's *presque vu.*

You had dreams about Ogden in the pointless seasons of adolescence. His sugary detestations, his heady denial of irrefutable things: his own birth, his own existence, the evidence of any anything but the opinions of certain clammering, hallucinated voices. It all appealed to you. In your dream, Ogden was a weepy, eccentric parody of Death himself. Death in a

jogging suit. Death, who cannot read a train schedule or tolerate heights.

You woke, read more, and dreamed again. You read Aspern the way others went to the refectory. You sat in a trunk and
did nothing but go through a stack of those narrow volumes
he produced irregularly. A bedpan alleviated difficulties. You
counted the wolf children among your relations. The world
was cleared of hypocrisy.

Best, you believed then, to make good on the love of
Aspern. You had so little of that. It had come to this. His
fragile constructions were yours, his barbarisms, too. He bent
to kill a wingless bird, to say what betrayal was; he made
overtures to livestock, spent time with his murderer, tripped
a girl on crutches. In his own words, he did. You sat in the
gabled window and howled, beat your chest. Not a stitch
adorned you, and, below, corduroys in many colors trotted
past, from Ethics to Engineering.

But you never wrote to him. It slipped your mind, gradually, casual victim of sloth.

Now his address, his point on the plane, sits on your desk,
a specimen for vivisection, or so you wish. It's not Venice,
Italy, but Venice, California; it's not a cubicle apartment in a
rooming house where a deaf woman serves him soup and
penicillin; it's the Grand Adams Luxury Apartments.

Between the perfidious chatter of the letter, images of
Aspern at play besiege you. Aspern on the tennis court, leaping gaily for a half volley. Aspern fly-fishing. Aspern with nou-
velle cuisine.

Put your head down. Hold yourself tightly. Proof from
math clubs, ham-radio frequencies, pornographic-magazine
kiosks attest, in your mercantile nation, to the fertility of the
Aspern legend. You are late to coo with the little woman, to
smack the back of your head with your hand and talk of small
pleasures overlooked.

This is not evidence of villainy or failure. Certainly not.
Could villainy or failure inhabit mere survival? **Q**

Sometimes, even when a friend does something terrible and dangerous, you can't stop to help him. There's nothing you can do. You just have to let him hurtle on past, and feel the breeze of his dumb passage.

Vern is doing it like a dance step: it's as if he's dancing with a very tall lady. Perhaps she is laughing at the bald spot, on the top of his head, as she looks down, and waltzes him into this new, familiar place of the ludicrous.

He's not a dumb man. But he has left his wife, and makes short angry chopping motions whenever he tells me—all too often—that it is cut off—finished—that he will never go back.

Austin is seven, Wejumtka, four. Vern's age really isn't important, is it? Wouldn't it look silly on the paper, just sitting there, like that?

So now he is single. Successively, there has been the apartment, and then the sports car, and then weak, feeble dates, which he tells me about, in horrendous detail.

He goes on and on about the car, too: about how it gives him *pleasure* to drive it. He raves about this car. Last week, on four separate occasions, he tells me, he came out of the grocery store, the cleaner's, wherever, and found somebody looking into the car: cupping their hands at the window. He stands up and demonstrates.

He doesn't fly on business trips anymore, he tells me, because he likes driving that car so much.

He talks about the car as if before it would not have been possible for him to have it and still be married.

Also, he has joined the aerobics class after work, an incident which I cannot even discuss.

He says that his children, Austin and Wejumtka, are killing him.

He says this as if it is something they mean to do to him.

But he does not make the quick chopping motions.

He looks down at his shoes.

We're over at my house, on a rainy day, a day off from work, and we're having beers. I found these huge filet mignons, three pounds, marked down for quick sale. I do all of my cooking, have for some time now, and I looked at those steaks, and bought them, and invited Vern over for the rainy day.

He says that Wejumtka takes hold of his fingers and looks in his eyes and tells him that he says his prayers, every night, for him to come home.

It was about seven years ago, when my wife and I first came to this city, that Vern had us over for dinner.

There were steaks then, too, and we all drank red wine, which was good. I seem to remember candles, though they may have been the artificial kind, plugged into a socket. It doesn't seem to matter. I remember that there was that kind of lighting: it might as well have been from real candles.

I was pretty young, both my wife and I were, and we were pretty easily impressed.

Vern's wife, Ann, had this old dark thin knife, with which she was doing something in the kitchen: coring lettuce, cutting cheese, something—I can't remember.

It was just an old piss-ant knife, one such as you might find in a garage sale, in a box with other things, for ten cents, or even a nickel.

They had a very nice home, and in the other room, we were eating with nice steak knives, fine dishes, and it must have embarrassed Ann for me to see her using that old thing, because she looked at it and began apologizing, almost immediately. She waved it around, flustered for no reason, explaining that it was just one of those things she had never bothered to throw away.

But I liked that knife, tremendously—the wooden handle

of it was stained with meat juices, from over the years, as was the blade—it was a knife you might see on a hunting trip, in a cabin—and we had been drinking very much wine, and I asked her if I could have the knife.

She was acting a little hysterical in the kitchen, I thought, as if she meant to throw it out that night.

Everyone thought I was nuts, and we laughed and talked about it and made fun of me for the rest of the night.

I remember driving home in silence with my wife that night, late, a long drive, with an odd silence, almost the beginning of a tension between us, and it could have been because of the knife.

Of course we had been drinking—but, still, something seemed to be troubling her, which neither of us could define.

Vern says that the best thing, the most absolute best thing about the aerobics class—and he is in the honesty of his beer now, looking very sad, so sad—despite his new car—is that the class puts him home at seven o'clock instead of five-thirty.

He had the kids over for Thanksgiving. They arrived at ten o'clock in the morning, and had to go home at seven. It was the first day they had come over to his apartment. It was the first day of the arrangement, of what Ann and Vern and Ann's lawyer and Vern's lawyer had worked out.

Austin, the older one, took his father's hand this time. It was exactly seven o'clock, Vern told me.

"Dad, is this the way it's going to be?" he asked his father.

He wasn't so much worried as just unsure. All he wanted to know was what was what.

"Is this the way it's going to be?" He kept looking up, Vern said, sort of walking around him, holding on to his hand, and asking: "I want to know—is this how it's going to be?"

Somebody should tell him.
Vern, I mean.

They are not divorced yet—just separated. Somebody should let him know.

But there is nothing I can do.

It's really more of a cabin, where I live now; it is far out in the country. It is a day in the country to come out and visit me.

We stood around in the kitchen, drinking beers—and, as it was raining, I did the steaks in a little skillet, in some butter, sprinkling them with pepper. We stood around and just watched them, and I kept turning them.

The little house is pretty bare. A lot of my spoons are plastic, from Wendy's. I don't need much: a skillet, a pot. None of the silverware, if you want to call it that, matches. But it doesn't matter.

The steaks were getting ready, and Vern was standing there talking, really down, and drinking those beers.

I saw that knife, in the drawer.

It was one of only two I had which would be suitable. The other one was serrated, and would work nicely also.

It wasn't as if he would have to use that particular knife.

But one of us would. He would have to watch me use it if he didn't.

I looked at those pretty steaks, ready to eat now, and hot, and I gave Vern that knife.

Then we stood there at the counter, as I have no table, and we ate, standing up, and I watched, detached but also slightly sick to my stomach, as he cut into the meat.

It was as if he were cutting into himself. It was as if he wasn't even aware of it. I kept thinking that at any second it would start to hurt: him cutting that steak.

The steak was meaty and red, and it looked like a human heart. Juices came from it. It didn't make any sense, why there was no pain. It looked like his heart. **Q**

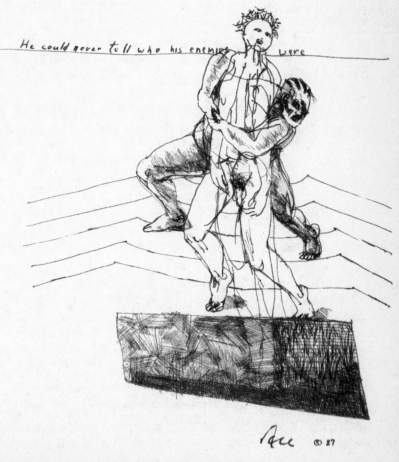

He could never tell who his enemies were